G++ 15.00

PLEASURES AND TREASURES

FINE BOOKS

For Ella

'Love, sweetness, goodness, in her person shin'd
So clear, as in no face with more delight'

ALAN G. THOMAS

FINE BOOKS

G. P. PUTNAM'S SONS
NEW YORK

Acknowledgements

The following illustrations are reproduced by kind permission of the Trustees or librarians concerned:

British Museum: 3, 4, 5, 8, 11, 12, 13, 14, 15, 17, 19, 21, 28, 30, 33, 34, 35, 36, 39, 40, 41, 42, 43, 46, 47, 48, 49, 50, 52, 53, 54, 55, 56, 58, 59, 60, 61, 62, 63, 65, 66, 73, 74, 76, 77, 78, 79, 80, 81, 82, 83, 84, 85, 86, 87, 88, 89, 90, 91, 92, 93, 94, 95, 96, 97, 98, 102, 108, 109; Trinity College, Dublin: 7, 16; Biblioteca Laurenziana, Florence: 18; John Rylands Library, Manchester: 45.

The following illustrations are from the collection of the author: 1, 2, 6, 9, 10, 20, 22, 23, 24, 25, 26, 27, 29, 31, 32, 37, 38, 44, 51, 57, 64, 67, 68, 69, 70, 72, 99, 100, 101, 103, 104, 105, 106, 107, 110, 111, 112, 113, 114, 115, 116, 117, 118, 119.

All the illustrations were specially photographed for this book by John Freeman and Co. Ltd, with the exception of the manuscripts in the British Museum, which were taken by the Museum photographers, and the following:

7, 16 (Green Studio, Dublin); title-page, 1, 2, 6, 9, 10, 20, 22, 23, 27, 29 (Studio Briggs); 45 (John Rylands Library); 18 (Biblioteca Laurenziana).

Printed in Germany by K. G. Lohse, Graphischer Grossbetrieb OHG,
Frankfurt am Main

Library of Congress Catalog Card Number: 67-21990

Contents

1 Franciscan or Dominican friars and parish priests carried small service books such as this in their wallets. In the calendar for December, a baker prepares bread in readiness for the grim medieval winter

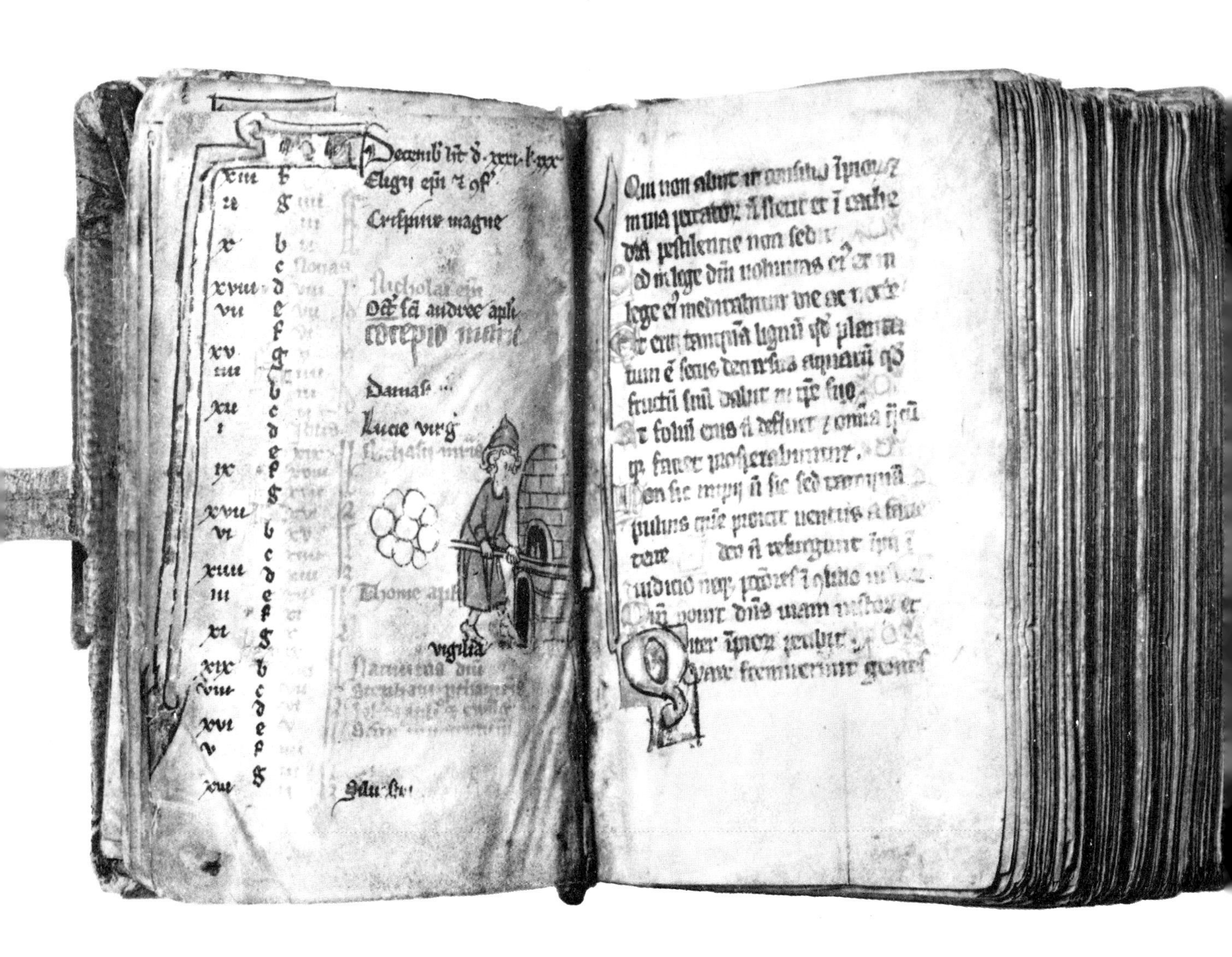

Preface

'OF MAKING MANY BOOKS there is no end,' wailed the Preacher. To what organ roll of prophetic lamentation would the author of Ecclesiastes have been inspired by the situation today? Nobody knows how many different books there are in the world, but their number has been estimated at over thirty million. If I were to deal with them all in the twenty thousand words available here the ratio would be about one word to every fifteen hundred books. Even the shortest sketch of the visual aspect of the book, in the space available, could amount to little more than a catalogue, a collection of dry bones. By selecting four aspects of European book production – Manuscripts, Early Printing, Colourplate Books and Private Presses – I hope to give some details of interest, some human anecdotes: to add flesh, as it were, to the skeleton. So if there is a jump from the early fifteenth to the late eighteenth century it is not because I am blind to the splendid books that were created at other times: atlases, early herbals, and natural history books with fine coloured plates. Nor have I touched upon that most sophisticated of all groups, French illustrated books of the eighteenth century, or the brilliant *livres à peinture* produced under the aegis of Vollard, let alone the infinite variety of bookbinding.

None the less, the books described here range from the Lindisfarne Gospels written in the seventh century to the private presses, many of which only closed down under the impact of the last war.

2 This initial comes from a volume recording the feudal privileges of the De Facla family, written in North Italy, perhaps Padua, late in the fifteenth century. The candelabrum is identical with one carried on high in Mantegna's *Triumph of Scipio* (now in the National Gallery, London)

The manuscripts give a wonderful conspectus of man's attempt over the centuries to give visual expression to the light within; the colour plate books, his efforts to recapture the beauty of the visual world; the printed books, his progress in giving dignified expression to the intellect and spirit. However inadequate my treatment may be, at least the subject represents one of the most glorious achievements of Western civilization.

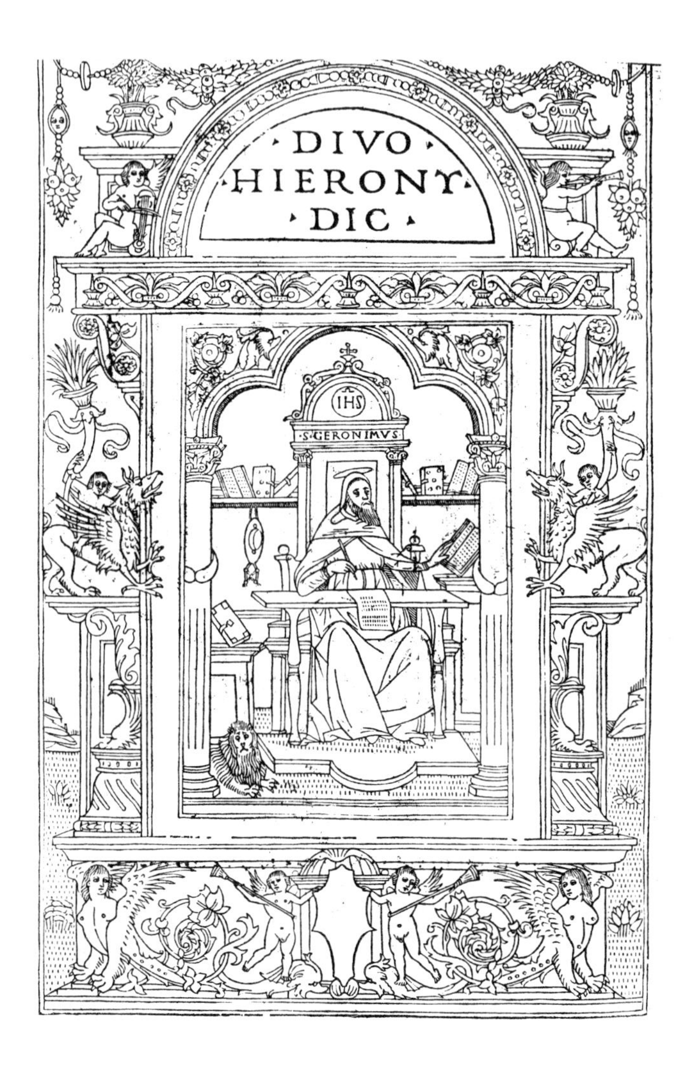

3 A woodcut from an edition of St Jerome's *Epistles*, printed in Ferrara in 1497 by Laurentius de Rubeis

4 *(opposite)* The central cross of the Gospels, written by Eadfrith, Bishop of Lindisfarne (Holy Island), in Northumbria, a little before 700 AD

imago homi nis :-
O AGIOS
MATT
heus

CHAPTER ONE

Manuscripts

IN THESE DAYS when the world is flooded with books, when in England alone about 23,000 new volumes are published every year, it is difficult to think oneself back into an age when there were not only no *printed* books, but very few books of any kind: when the great majority could neither read nor write. By the Dark Ages of the sixth century the barbarian hordes had swept across Europe, destroying both the classical world of Greece and Rome, and, to a great extent, the early Christian civilization. At this time nearly all educated men were in the Church, and indeed, our word 'clerk', one who earns his living with a pen, derives from 'cleric', a clergyman. A great many of these men, no doubt, were in the Church from a sense of vocation, but there were also many men who wanted a quiet and decent life in circumstances of comparative comfort. Today their spiritual descendants are to be found in the civil service and in broadcasting.

At this time the standards of peace and security, without which very little is achieved in this life, were most likely to be found in the monasteries, where dedicated men led a communal life; and the monasteries themselves might be compared with a chain of castles holding the line for the spiritual and intellectual life in a dark and savage land. Most religious houses possessed libraries, in which were preserved not only the Bible and the great texts of Christendom, but also, in some fortunate cases, the books

6 When Napoleon's soldiers invaded Italy they looted and cut up many fine manuscripts, including the one from which this miniature was taken. It was produced in Milan *c.* 1470, possibly for the Olivetans, by Venturino Mercati

5 *(opposite)* The angel, the traditional symbol for St Matthew, watches the Evangelist as he writes, in this portrait from the *Lindisfarne Gospels*

7 *(overleaf left)* The opening words of Matthew 1.18, from the *Book of Kells*, written on the Island of Iona in the second half of the eighth century – the supreme example of Celtic illumination

8 *(overleaf right)* The 'Beatus' page from an Anglo-Saxon Psalter, probably written at Canterbury in the early eleventh century

h generatio

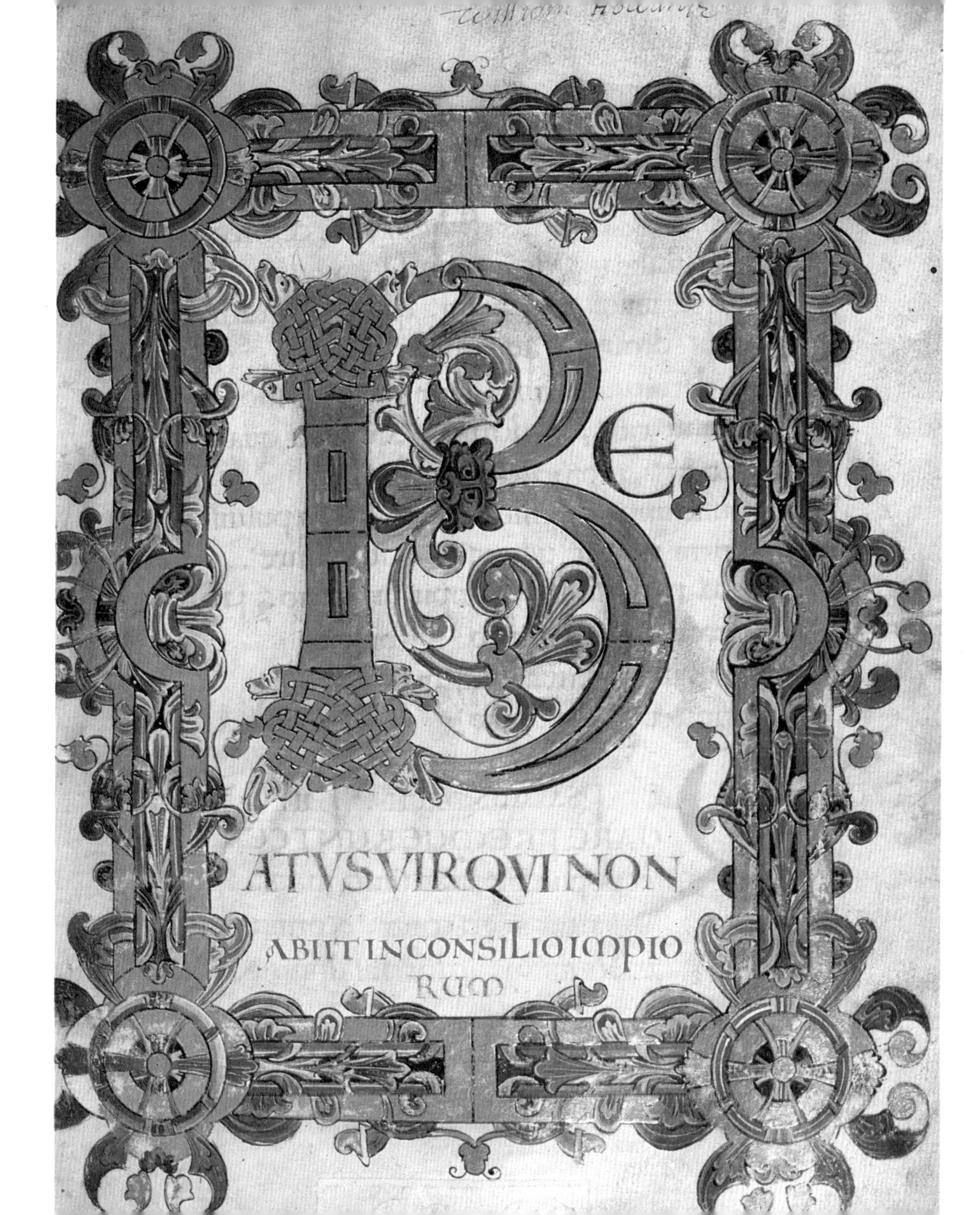
Be
ATUSUIRQUINON
ABIIT INCONSILIO IMPIO
RUM

9 In this fifteenth-century MS. the new world has arrived. Renaissance detail replaces Gothic ornament, a lay figure, very often the author, appears in the initial and the humanist script is ancestor to the printing types which we read every day

which contained practically everything which has come down to us from the ancient world in the way of spiritual teaching, philosophy, literature, history, medicine and science. Some works survived in many manuscripts; others, such as Catullus, in only one. Had some mischance destroyed this single volume we should never have heard the words: My sweetest Lesbia let us live and love.

Our debt to these men is incalculable. Let us now consider how they created these manuscripts. We are used to borrowing or even buying books without difficulty; but in those days a rich man or a wealthy institution would employ a scribe and an illuminator, perhaps for years on end, to write a book for them. And although there was already a flourishing book trade in Oxford by the twelfth century, the only course open to a poor scholar was to buy the necessary equipment and set to work himself; Chaucer's Clerk of Oxenford probably produced the 'twenty bokes, clad in blak or reed' which 'stodd above his beddes heed' in this way – though the thought of writing out the whole Bible single-handed must have seemed intimidating. Many such humble manuscripts are still in existence; I once owned a copy of the Sermons of St Augustine written by Stephen Dodesham, a visionary who died in 1482. This was signed and dated, 1462, in the Carthusian monastery at Witham; while another MS simply bore the anonymous and endearing note '*Unum ave maria pro scriptore*', a prayer for the scribe.

But in the early days, before the thirteenth century, the great majority of books must have been written in monasteries, and especially in Benedictine and Cistercian houses. The really great centres were comparatively few in number: in England – Winchester, St Albans, Canterbury, Durham, Glastonbury, Bury St Edmunds. The scriptorium in a Benedictine house was generally over the chapter-house, or perhaps the scribes worked in carrels in the cloister as at Gloucester. Strict rules were applied. Artificial light was forbidden for fear of fire; absolute silence was enjoined, and, to avoid the mistakes which so frequently follow interruption, only the highest monastic officials were allowed to enter the scriptorium. Communication was by signs: if a scribe needed a book he extended his hands and turned over imaginary leaves, a missal was signified by the sign of the cross, a psalter by placing the hands on the head in the shape of a crown (a reference to King David), a lectionary by wiping away imaginary grease fallen from candles, and a pagan work by scratching the body in the manner of a dog.

At first all books were written on vellum, the skin generally of sheep, goats or calves, washed, dressed and rubbed smooth. Smaller books or more delicate works were written on the finer uterine vellum which is the skin of a still-born calf or lamb. Vellum is one of the best materials ever used in book production; it is smooth, white, tough and lasting, the only disadvantage being its high cost. How many sheep, one speculates, would be needed for a single Bible?

Lines were ruled with a blunt scriber, making hollows on one side of the leaf, ridges on the other, the spacing of the lines having first been pricked out down each margin with an awl. The pen was a reed or quill, cut with a pen-knife; the ink was made of soot, gum and water, or, alternatively, galls, sulphate of iron and gum.

Scribes were held in high honour; it is always good to be able to do what nobody else can do. In Ireland in the seventh and eighth centuries the penalty for killing a scribe was equal to that for killing a bishop, and it was considered an honour to St Patrick himself that he was so good a scribe.

The mention of St Patrick brings us to an interesting and curious situation; while the rest of Europe wallowed in the Dark Ages Ireland was a blaze of light; the barbarians exhausted their impetus attacking England, and Ireland was left in peace. From that peace there emerged one of those inexplicable creative periods in history similar to those of England under Elizabeth or Florence under the Medici. Scholarship flourished and Europeans travelled to Ireland in

10 The cares of his flock sit heavily on the shoulders of this gorgeously robed sainted bishop depicted in a North Italian Antiphoner of the fifteenth century

11, 12 *(overleaf)* The mode of travel of the ruling classes in the fourteenth century is delightfully presented in these pages from the *Luttrell Psalter*, one of the prime sources of our knowledge of English medieval life

tum nostrum
Recordatus est quoniam puluis
sumus: homo sicut fenum dies eius
tanquam flos agri sic efflorebit.
Quoniam spiritus pertransibit in
illo ⁊ non subsistet: ⁊ non cognoscet
amplius locum suum
Misericordia autem domini ab eter
no: ⁊ usque in eternum super timen
tes eum
Et iusticia illius in filios filiorū:
his qui seruant testamentum eius.
Et memores sunt mandatorum
ipsius: ipsius: ad faciendum ea.

Dominus in celo parauit sedem su
am: ⁊ regnum ipsius omnibus do
minabitur.
Benedicite domino omnes angeli
eius potentes uirtute facientes uer
bum illius: ad audiendam uocem
sermonum eius.
Benedicite domino omnes uirtu
tes eius: ministri eius qui facitis
uoluntatem eius.
Benedicite domino omnia opera
eius: in omni loco dominacionis
eius benedic anima mea domino.
Benedic anima mea domi

order to learn Greek, which, when one considers what travel must have been like in the dark ages, is no mean tribute to Irish civilization.

From Christian Ireland missionaries set out to re-convert pagan Europe to the faith, and at each stage on the journey they founded a monastery in which books were produced: first Iona in Scotland and Lindisfarne in northern England, then through what is now Germany and Switzerland to St Gall, and across the Alps to Italy, where they founded a monastery famous for its manuscripts at Bobbio.

In 635 King Oswald invited St Aidan to come from Iona as missionary to Northumbria; he made his head-quarters on Holy Island, or Lindisfarne, where he founded a monastery on an Irish plan. Here, a little before 700 AD, was produced the most splendid surviving example of Northumbrian illumination, the Lindisfarne Gospels. About two hundred and fifty years later Aldred, son of Alfred and Tilwin, added a gloss in English, and, fortunately for us, wrote a note about the origin of the book, which, for a brief moment, draws aside the curtain which hides the life on that stormswept island. 'Eadfrith, Bishop of the church of Lindisfarne, he at the first wrote this book for God and for St Cuthbert and for the whole company of the saints whose relics are on the island. And Ethilwald, Bishop of those of Lindisfarne island, bound and covered it outwardly as well as he could. And Billfrith the anchorite he wrought, as a smith, the ornaments that are on the outside and adorned it with gold and with gems and gilded silver, unalloyed metal. And Aldred, an unworthy and most miserable priest, with God's help and St Cuthbert's, overglossed it in English' etc. Figure 4 reproduces folio 26. The central cross is surrounded by an interlacing pattern of incredible complexity, completely Celtic in feeling, an early example of the perverse delight in complication for its own sake that is still to be found, over twelve hundred years later, in the works of James Joyce. It is carried out with craftsmanship of breath-taking accuracy, every twist and interlacing of the complex pattern being depicted in perfect detail; heads of fantastic animals bite the ribbons as they go by, while the subtle colour sense may well be described as magical. Figure 5 depicts the portrait of St Matthew which faces the opening of his Gospel.

One aspect of the Lindisfarne Gospels bears fascinating witness to the international character of the Church in those early days; for – about the last thing one would have imagined – liturgically it is Neapolitan. Benedict Biscop, a Northumbrian nobleman who founded the twin monasteries of Wearmouth-Jarrow, made more than one journey to Italy and brought back manuscripts from Vivarium, that great centre of Benedictine book production founded by Cassiodorus; while Bede tells us that Hadrian, Abbot of Nisita near Naples, who later spent some years at Canterbury, came on a mission to Northumbria in 669; and the liturgy of the Lindisfarne Gospels was doubtless influenced by the activities of these two men. In 875 the Danes invaded Lindisfarne and destroyed the monastery; indeed there was no further monastic life there until it was refounded by a Norman Bishop of Durham more than 200 years later. The monks fled, carrying their more portable treasures, including the relics of St Cuthbert and this book. It was carried from place to place, and during a journey to Ireland was washed overboard in a storm but recovered miraculously uninjured at low tide. One is reminded of Mr Eldridge Johnson, a keen American yachtsman who once owned the original manuscript of *Alice in Wonderland*; loath to be parted from his treasure, yet fearful of its safety, he took it to sea in a specially constructed waterproof box which was guaranteed to float away in safety should his yacht sink.

After many wanderings, the Lindisfarne Gospels came to rest in Durham, where they were seen in the twelfth century by a certain Simeon of Durham, as he records in his history of the cathedral. But in all probability the book was later returned to the refounded priory on Lindisfarne, for the in

13 The Island of Iona, from Daniell's *Voyage Round Great Britain* (see page 94). It was in simple buildings such as these, in a setting of natural grandeur, that many of the finest early manuscripts were written

14 *(overleaf left)* This thirteenth-century *Biblia Latina* was written for Robertus de Bello, Abbot of Canterbury. The Book of Genesis opens with a long initial I, containing the seven days of Creation, with six other scenes in the roundels at the foot of the page

15 *(overleaf right)* The *Luttrell Psalter*, 'East Anglian School'; Sir Geoffrey Luttrell, of Irnham in Lincolnshire, who commissioned this manuscript in about 1335-40, is seen with his wife and daughter-in-law

[Ge]nesis

IN PRINCIPIO CREAVIT DEUS

celum et terram. Terra autem erat ina
nis et vacua et tenebre erant sup faciem a
bissi et spc dni ferebatur sup aquas. Dixitq;
deus. fiat lux. Et fca est lux. Et vidit deus lu
cem qd eet bona: et divisit lucem ac tenebris.
Appellavitq; lucem diem et tenebras noctem
factumq; est vespe et mane dies unus. Dix
quoq; deus. fiat firmamentum in medio
aquar et dividat aquas ab aquis. Et fecit de
firmamentum divisitq; aquas que erat
sup firmamentu ab his que erant sub fir
mamento. Et fcm est ita. Vocavitq; firma
mentum deus celum. Et fcm est vespe et ma
ne dies scds. Dixit vero deus. Congregentur
aque que sub celo sunt in locum unum:
et appareat arida. fcmq; est ita. Et vocavit ds
aridam terram: congregationesq; aquar
appellavit maria. Et vidit deus q eet bon
et ait. Germinet terra herbam virentem et
facientem semen et lignum pomifer faci
ens fructu iuxta genus suum. cui semen i
semet ipso sit sup terram. Et fcm est ita. Et p
tulit tra herbam virentem et afferentem sem
iuxta genus suum. lignumq; faciens fruc
tu et hns unumqdq; sementem scdm specie
suam. Et vidit ds q eet bonum et fcm est ve
spe et mane dies tercius. Dixit autem deus. fiat
luminaria in firmamento celi ut dividat
diem ac noctem et sint in signa et tempora et
dies et annos ut luceant in firmamento celi et
illuminent terram. Et fcm est ita. fecitq; ds
duo magna luminaria: luminare mai ut pre
esset diei et luminare min ut peet nocti. Et
stellas. Et posuit eas in firmamento celi ut lu
cerent sup terram et peent diei ac nocti. ut di
viderent lucem ac tenebras. Et vidit deus qd
eet bonum: et fcm est vespe et mane dies qrt.
Dixit et ds. Producant aque reptile aie viventis
et volatile sup terram: sub firmamento celi
Creavitq; deus cete grandia et omem animam

pudore: ⁊ operiantur sicut diploide
confusione sua
Confitebor domino nimis in
ore meo: et in medio multorum
laudabo eum
Qui astitit a dextris pauperis:
ut saluam faceret a persequentibꝫ
animam meam.
Gloria patri
Dn̄s Galfridus louterell me fieri
fecit

ventory of 1367 records: '*Liber S. Cuthberti qui demersus in mare.*' After the sack of the monasteries the manuscript disappears from our ken, until in the seventeenth century it was acquired by Sir Robert Cotton (stripped of its jewelled binding), and passed, with his library, to the British Museum on its foundation in 1753.

'That man is little to be envied,' said Dr Johnson, 'whose patriotism would not gain force upon the plain of Marathon, or whose piety would not grow warmer among the ruins of Iona!' It was here, in 563, that St Columba founded the monastery which rapidly became the centre of Celtic Christianity and which sent forth missionaries to pagan Europe. And it was here in the second half of the eighth century that the supreme masterpiece of the Celtic school, one of the world's greatest books, was written – the *Book of Kells*. A few years later the Abbot Cellach and his monks, fleeing from the Norsemen, and carrying the unfinished manuscript with them, took refuge in the Abbey of Kells about forty miles from Dublin. Here the precious book remained until it was given to Trinity College, Dublin, in the seventeenth century. It contains the four Gospels decorated with an unusual wealth of illumination, all but two of the pages being painted. Experts have detected the work of four different artists of unequal talent, and an exceptionally wide series of European and Near-Eastern influences. It is hopeless to summarize a book of such richness in the few words available to me here, except, perhaps, to make one point. In the Lindisfarne Gospels the upsurging Celtic imagination is kept within almost classical control as if the wild romantic spirit were held within the Roman discipline of the Catholic Church. In the *Book of Kells* there is far less restraint; the Irish temperament is given free rein.

The exuberance of the *Book of Kells* is well displayed in the three opening words of Matthew 1.18, '*Christi autem generatio*', with '*Christi* (XPI)' and '*autem*' contracted [figure 7]. Irish scholars, and who can contradict them,

16 *(opposite)* Portrait of an Evangelist from the *Book of Kells*, Iona, second half of the eighth century

claim that this is 'the most elaborate specimen of calligraphy which has ever existed'. Towards the left-hand side, almost hidden in the pattern, there are three angels, two of whom hold books, while the third grasps a pair of blossoming sceptres with all his might, as if he were frightened lest the swirling pattern in which they have become entangled were about to snatch them out of his hands. Crouching under the tail of the P, a couple of rats are surreptitiously nibbling at the Host, while two cats, with reprehensible languor, look on. There is some dispute as to whether figure 16 represents Christ, St Mark or St Luke, but I feel fairly certain that one of the Evangelists is depicted. Although the greater part of this splendid page is of the highest quality, it seems to have been completed by a lesser hand; for whereas the detail in the top left corner is equal to the superb work of the main frame, the other three corners and the two roundels are distinctly inferior.

For those who do not live in Dublin, whose fortunate inhabitants can see a different page of the *Book of Kells* every day, there is a first-rate facsimile in colour, published by Urs Graf of Berne.

The Amiatino Bible is not only the most important codex of the vulgate in existence but also the supreme example of English uncial writing, its splendid script marching majestically across the pages like the assured tramp of the Roman legions. It was written in the twin monasteries of Wearmouth-Jarrow, the home of the Venerable Bede, the heart of Northumbrian civilization. The Abbot Ceolfrid commissioned three copies of the Bible, one for each of the monasteries, another as a present for the Pope. Armed with his precious burden he set out for Rome in 716 but died on the journey, without having accomplished his mission. The Bible passed into other hands, which, one blushes to add, faked the presentation inscription by erasing the words *Ceolfridus* and *Anglorum* and substituting *Petrus* and *Langobardorum*. The book remained on Mount Amiata until the monastery was

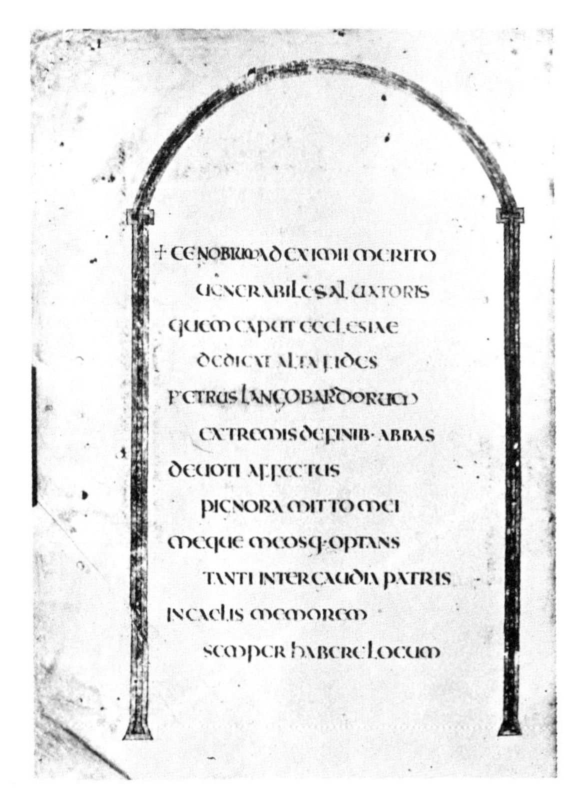

+CENOBIUM AD EXIMII MERITO
UENERABILE SALUATORIS
QUEM CAPUT ECCLESIAE
DEDICAT ALTA FIDES
PETRUS LANGOBARDORUM
EXTREMIS DE FINIB· ABBAS
DEUOTI AFFECTUS
PIGNORA MITTO MEI
MEQUE MEOSQ· OPTANS
TANTI INTER GAUDIA PATRIS
IN CAELIS MEMOREM
SEMPER HABERE LOCUM

18 The *Codex Amiatinus*, Northumbria, eighth century. The faking in the fifth line can be clearly seen, the name '*Petrus Langobardorum*' written over the space where that of the Abbot Ceolfrid had been erased

17 *(opposite) Carmelite Missal*, English, fourteenth century. The Emperor Heraclius and his courtiers wear the fashionable clothes of the period of King Richard II; it was formerly held that this was indeed a portrait of that monarch

supressed in 1782 when it passed to its final home, the Biblioteca Laurenziana in Florence. The fraudulent inscription remained undetected and the book was assumed to be Italian until it was examined, in the 1880s, by the great scholar Giovanni Battista de Rossi. Not only was the deception unravelled, but F.J.A. Hort discovered that the verses which head the codex were identical with those recorded by the eighth-century *Historia Abbatum* as having been inscribed in Ceolfrid's Bible. The other two manuscripts probably remained at Wearmouth and Jarrow until the suppression of the monasteries, when so many fine books perished. But in 1909 Canon Greenwell of Durham, browsing in a Newcastle bookshop in the neighbourhood of Jarrow, found a single leaf from one of them; the writing was not as faultless and may have been a trial run before perfection was achieved, but the family likeness was unmistakable. He gave his *trouvaille* to the British Museum. Since then ten further leaves, almost certainly from the same manuscript, have been discovered at Wollaton Hall, Nottinghamshire, where, in the sixteenth century, they were used as the covers for cartularies of lands belonging to the Willoughby family. The text comes from the third and fourth Book of Kings, the verses being arranged in the same way as in the *Codex Amiatinus*. They have also passed to the British Museum, where, and one is glad to learn of a man reaping his reward in an unjust world, they are known as the Ceolfrid Bible [figure 18].

The Northumbrian civilization, which did so much towards relighting the lamps all over Europe, was overrun and destroyed by the Danes, and we must turn to the Anglo-Saxon world of Southern England. Here a distinguished group of kings, bishops and abbots promoted a remarkable revival. This only lasted a little more than a hundred years, beginning with the accession of King Edgar in 959 and ending at Hastings in 1066. One of the most important elements in this upsurge was a revival of monasticism which found expression in the production of splendid manuscripts, especially at Winchester and Canterbury, generally known as the Winchester School. Figure 8, Arundel MS 155 in the British Museum, reproduces a psalter written, most probably, at Canterbury between 1012 and 1023.

King David gave medieval illuminators great opportunities by beginning the Psalms with the letter B (*Beatus Vir qui non abiit in consilio impiorum*) and the 'Beatus Page' is a great feature in many splendid MSS. The popular conception of the Saxons at the time of the Norman Conquest is of a lot of louts with tow-coloured hair wearing belted tunics and held down by an élite of semi-fascist house-carls – and yet they could produce works like this, superior to anything being done on the Continent at the time. Arundel MS 155 was later in the possession of Lord William Howard, 'The Wizard Earl', (whose signature is at the top of the page reproduced), but is now in the British Museum.

The first manuscripts to have survived in any quantity, and to be still available in private hands on a considerable scale, are the Bibles written, especially in France, during the hundred years following 1175. Europe had settled down to some extent after the Dark Ages; the strong hand of Philip Augustus, 1180-1223, had effected a considerable degree of security in France, enabling the arts of peace to flourish and Paris to assume that position as the intellectual capital of Europe which she has so often held since. With the reign of St Louis, 1226-70, the Middle Ages reached the apogee of artistic achievement and spiritual fervour. Universities were founded and flourished, while friars of the mendicant orders were to be seen in every market place.

All of this created a far greater demand for books than had ever existed before, but whereas most previous manuscripts had been written in monasteries, production now passed mainly to commercial workshops, which were to be found around the universities in Paris and elsewhere. However, a few really superb manuscripts were still produced in

19 A thirteenth-century Psalter. Psalm 80: *Exultate Deo, adjutori nostro: jubilate Deo Jacob* – Sing aloud unto God our strength: make a joyful noise unto the God of Jacob. King David strikes music from a row of bells with hammers

monasteries. Such was the international character of the monastic orders that monks moved not only from house to house but from country to country. Thus the great Bible which at one time belonged to St Loup de Troyes (and which now forms MSS 7-9 in the Bibliothèque Ste-Geneviève) bears the name of a scribe. He calls himself Manerius, asserts that his parents were a certain Wigmund and Leobgifu, and adds that he was Canterbury bred. When an English monk writes a manuscript in a French religious house, is it French or English? I usually call it 'Channel School'.

Robertus de Bello was abbot of St Augustine's, Canterbury, from 1224 to 1253, and his Bible [figure 14] was probably written there. The book of Genesis opens with a long initial I which extends the full length of the page and contains a series of roundels depicting the Days of Creation. The opening words, IN PRINCIPIO CREAVIT DEUS, are embodied in the illumination, while there are six more roundels, with scenes from Genesis, at the foot of the page. The more elaborate Bibles contain similar historiated initials throughout, the style and colouring of which bear a strong resemblance to the stained glass windows at Chartres and Sens. Indeed some authorities maintain that the artists who illuminated the manuscripts also designed the stained glass windows; but this idea is beyond proof, for we hardly know a single one of their names. The Bible of Robertus de Bello is a fairly typical example of mid-thirteenth-century work. Hundreds of similar Bibles may still be seen in almost any important library.

But in addition to the splendid books treasured by wealthy institutions and private patrons an immense quantity of quite humble Bibles poured from the workshops. These were modest in size, more sparsely illuminated, and generally written in a tiny, but neat and regular, script: compact books which fitted into the wallets of the wandering preachers and provided the texts for those sermons that were to have so significant an influence on European civilization.

20 *(opposite)* The figure of St John the Evangelist stands at the head of his Gospel in a small Bible written about 1250. He holds his symbol of an eagle

In principio erat ubu et ubu e
rat ap dm et deus erat ubu. Hoc
erat in principio ap dm. Oia p
ipm fca sunt: et sin ipo fcm e
nich. Qd fcm e i ipo uita erat.
et uita erat lux hom. Et lux i
tenebris lucet: et tenebre ea n
apprehenderunt. Fuit homo miss
a do: cui nom erat iohs. H uenit
i testimonium: ut testimoniu phibe
de lumie. ut oms crederent p illu. Non
erat ille lux: s3 ut testimoniu p
hiberet de lumie. Erat lux uera q illu
minat omem hoiem uenientem
i hunc mundu. In mundo erat et
mundus per ipm fcs e. et mund
eu n cognouit. In ppria uenit
et sui eu n receperunt. Quot
aut receperunt eum dedit eis potes
tatem filios di fieri his qui credunt
i noie eius. Qui n ex sanguinib3
ne3 ex uoluntate carnis ne3 ex
uoluntate uiri. s3 ex do nati st.
Et ubu caro fcm e. et habitauit
i nob. Et uidimus gl'am eius
gl'am qsi unigeniti a patre. ple
nu gre et ueritatis. Iohs testimo
niu phibet de ipo. et clamat di
cens. H erat qm dixi. qui p me
uenturus e ante me fcs e. qa prior
me erat. Et de plenitudine eius nos
oms accepim. et grm p gra. qa lex
p moysen data e. gra aut et ueritas
p ihm xpm fca e. Dm nemo uidit
unqm. Unigenitus filius qui e in
sinu pris ipe enarrauit. Et hoc e testi
monium iohis qn miserunt iudei ab
ierl'imis sacerdotes et leuitas ad eum
ut interrogarent eum. Tu quis es. Et
confessus e: et n negauit. Et confessus e
qa n sum ego xps. Et interrogauert eu.
Quid g. helias es tu. Et dixit. Non sum.
Propheta es tu. Et rndit. n. Dixerunt g ei.
Quis es: ut rsum demus his qui
miserunt nos. Quid dicis de te ipo. Ait.
Ego uox clamantis in deserto. dirigi
te uiam dni sic dixit ysaias pphta. Et
qui missi fuerant: ex phariseis erant. Et
interrogauerunt eu et dixerunt ei. Quid g
baptizas si tu n es xps. ne3 helias. ne3
pphta. Rndit eis iohs dicens. Ego bap
tizo in aq. medius aut ur̄m stetit qm
uos nescitis. Ipse e qui post me uentu
rus est. qui ante me fcs est. cui ego n

sum dignus ut soluam eius corrigi
am calciamti. H in bethania fca sunt tns
iordanem ubi erat iohs baptizans. Al
tera die uidit iohs ihm uenientem ad
se et ait. Ecce agnus di. ecce qui tollit
pecca mundi. Hic e de quo dixi. Post
me uenit uir qui ante me fcs e qa
prior me erat. Et ego nesciebam eum.
S3 ut manifestetur i isrl. pptea ueni e
go in aq baptizans. Et testimoniu p
hibuit iohs dicens. qa uidi spm qsi co
lumbam descendentem de celo et ma
nentem sr eum. Et ego nesciebam eu. S3 q
misit me baptizare i aq: ille m dixit.
Sr quem uideris spm descendentem et ma
nentem sr eum. h e qui baptizat i spu
sco et igni. Et ego uidi et testimoniu
phibui qa hic e filius dei. Altera die itm
stabat iohs et ex discipulis eius duo. et
respiciens ihm ambulantem dicit. Ecce
agnus dei. Et audierunt eu duo di
scipuli loquentem et secuti sunt ihm. Co
uersus aut ihs et uidens eos sequentes
se. dic eis. Quid queritis. Qui dixerunt.
Rabbi qd dr interptatum magr ubi hab
itas. Dic eis. Uenite et uidete. Uenerunt et ui
derunt ubi maneret. et manserunt ap illu
die illo. hora aut erat qsi x. Erat aut an
dreas frr symonis petri. unus ex duob
qui audierant a iohe et secuti fuerant
eum. Inuenit h primu frem suu sy
monem et dic ei. Inuenim messia
qd est interptatum xps. et adduxit eu ad
ihm. Intuitus aut ihs eu. dix. Tu es
symon filius iohanna. tu uocaberis
cephas qd intptr petrus. In crastinu
uoluit exire in galileam. et inuenit phi
lippum. et dic ei ihs. Sequere me. Erat
philippus a bethsaida. ciuitate andree
et petri. Inuenit philipp nathanael
et dixit ej. Que scripsit moyses i le
ge et pphe inuenim ihm filiu ioseph
a nazareth. Et dix ei nathanael. A na
zareth potest aliquid boni ee. Dic ei
philippus. Ueni et uide. Uidit ihs natha
nael uenientem ad se et dic de eo. Ec
ce uere isrlita i quo dolus n e. Dic
ei nathanael. Unde me nosti. Rndit ihs
et dic ei. Priusqm philippus te uocaret
cu esses sub ficu: uidi te. Rndit ei nathana
el et ait. Rabi tu es filius di. tu es rex
isrl. Rndit ihs et dixit ei. Quia dixi ti
bi te sub ficu. credis. maius his ui
debis. Et dic ei. Amen amen dico uobis uide

bitis celum apertum et angelos di ascen
dentes et descendentes sr filium hois.

Et die tertia nuptie fce sunt i
chana galilee et erat mr ihu ibi. Uo
catus e autem ihs et discipli eius ad
nuptias. Et deficiente uino dic mr ihu
ad eum. Uinu n habent. Dic ei ihs. Qd
m et tibi e mulier. nondu uenit hora mea. Dic mr
eius ministris. Quodcuq dixerit uob facite.
Erant autem ibi lapidee ydrie sex posi
te scdm purificationem iudeor capientes
singule metretas binas uel ternas. Dic eis
ihs. Implete ydrias aq. Et impleuer
eas usq ad sumu. Et dic eis ihs. Haurite
nunc et ferte architriclino. Et tuler.
Ut aut gustauit architriclinus aqm uinu
fcam. et n sciebat unde eet. ministri aut sci
ebant qui hauserant aqm. uocat spo
sum architriclinus et dic ei. Omis ho
primu bonu uinu ponit. et cu inebriati
fuerint tunc id qd deterius est. Tu aut seruasti
bonu uinu usq ad huc. Hoc fecit initiu
signor ihs in chana galilee. et manife
stauit gl'am sua. Et crediderunt i eu dis
cipuli eius. Post h descendit capharnau
ipse et mr eius et fres eius et discipli eius
et ibi manserunt n multis diebus. Et ppe
erat pascha iudeor. et ascendit ihs ierli
mam. et inuenit in templo uendentes
oues et boues et columbas et nummula
rios sedentes. Et cu fecisset qsi flagellu
de funiculis oms eiecit de templo. Oues
quoq et boues. et nummulariorum effudit
es et mensas subuertit. Et his qui colum
bas uendebant dixit. Auferte ista
hinc et nolite facere domu pris mei domu ne
gociationis. Recordati sunt discipli eius
qa scptu e. Zelus domus tue comedit me.
Rnderunt g iudei et dixerunt ei. Quod signu
ostendis nob. qa hec facis. Rndit ihs et dix
eis. Soluite templu hoc. et in trib die
bus excitabo illud. Dixerunt g ei iudei. Qua
draginta et sex annis edificatum e templu hoc. et
tu in trib diebus excitabis illud. Ille aut
dicebat de templo corporis sui. Cu g
resurrexisset a mortuis. recordati sunt
discipuli eius qa hoc dicebat de corpo
re suo. et crediderunt scripture et sermoni q
dixit eis ihs. Cu aut eet ierosolimis i
pascha i die festo multi crediderunt i no
mine eius uidentes signa eius que fa
ciebat. Ipse aut ihs n credebat se semetipm
eis. eo qd ipe nosset omes. et qa opus ei n e
rat ut quis testimoniu phiberet de

Probably the favourite book before the appearance of the Breviary and the Book of Hours was the Psalter, some of the richest of which were produced by the so-called East Anglian School. I use this phrase because no better definition has received general acceptance. It has been employed in the past because many of the most important examples are connected with Norfolk: the Gorleston, Ramsey, St Omer, Ormesby and other Psalters. But even its firmest advocates are forced to extend East Anglia by the inclusion of Peterborough, and it seems probable now that some of the major Psalters were produced in other parts of the country. East Anglia was then a rich and flourishing centre of agriculture and the wool trade; populous towns existed and great churches were built where there are now a few cottages.

By this time production of the more sumptuous MSS, at any rate those commissioned by wealthy lay patrons, had passed out of the hands of monks and the books were created in commercial workshops. These Psalters were planned on a large scale and the spacious margins gave full opportunity to the riotous imagination of the illuminators. In addition to religious pictures there were fabulous beasts and vigorous scenes from daily life: bear-baiting, juggling, ploughing, sowing, harrowing, harvesting, cooking and feasting; they were a sort of fourteenth-century illustrated journal, to be idly leafed through when wet weather confined ladies to the castle or manor. The *magnum opus* is the Luttrell Psalter, whose pictures have become especially well known over the last eighty or so years with the spread of that interest in the history of everyday life promoted by John Richard Green, J. J. Jusserand, Marjorie and C.H.B. Quennell, G.M. Trevelyan and others; and there can be few people blessed with any feeling for history whose childhood imagination was not quickened by the illustrations in such books. Figure 15 depicts Sir Geoffrey Luttrell, of Irnham in Lincolnshire, who commissioned the manuscript about 1335-40, accompanied by his wife and daughter-in-law; Eric Millar, in his learned monograph, described this as 'an early example of an English conversation piece'. In figures 11 & 12 the artist has depicted a coach for four queens, a sort of precursor of the royal train; a small chest which may well be a tool-box hangs underneath; the horses have spiked shoes like athletes. There is some doubt whether Sir Geoffrey actually received the manuscript, for the decoration was not entirely completed, and certain portions are by a much inferior hand.

A book which, in its time, must have been among the most beautiful of English manuscripts was the Missal written during the late fourteenth century for the Carmelites of Whitefriars, London [figures 17 & 21]. Certain portions of this already imperfect book came into the possession of Philip Augustus Hanrott, an early nineteenth-century collector who had the good fortune to inhabit one of the lovely houses built by the Adam brothers in the Adelphi. His children, believe it or not, cut up the Missal to make scrapbooks, sticking in the better pictures and spelling out their own names with a series of illuminated initials; a title-page was spelt out with further fragments: INITIAL LETTERS. The younger ones made further scrapbooks from the 'left-overs', while the text and humbler fragments of decoration were thrown away. At the Hanrott sale in 1833 the major scrapbooks were acquired by Sir William Tite, soon after whose death in 1873 they passed to the British Museum. Here the scrapbooks remained intact, greatly admired and often exhibited, until 1933, when an American scholar, Margaret Rickert, conceived the idea of reconstructing the Missal from the surviving fragments. The solution of this colossal jigsaw puzzle took about five years, most of the clues coming from such fragments of text as survived on the backs of the scraps. Numerous liturgical scholars lent their aid; Neil Ker identified another scrapbook in the library of Glasgow University; and then, one day in September 1936, two sisters, members of the Hanrott family, turned up at the British Museum with yet another scrapbook bearing the name of

21 The Missal written for the Carmelites in London in the fourteenth century was desecrated in the nineteenth, when children were allowed to cut out the initials to make scrap books. Inside this initial letter T, a bishop is conducting the ceremony for the dedication of a church, while Christ, detached from the worldly plane and painted high up in the margin, looks down in blessing

22 St Helena was the mother of Constantine, the first Christian Roman Emperor. At a great age she visited the Holy Land where, traditionally, she discovered the True Cross, which she is seen holding in this miniature from a breviary written in Ferrara about 1460

23 *(opposite)* In this decorated opening page of the Vespers for the Dead, from a Book of Hours produced during the second half of the fifteenth century in Florence, we can see how quickly the new Renaissance floral vocabulary matured

Ellen A. Hanrott spelt out the same way with illuminated initials. Ellen Hanrott, a younger daughter, had been left to make do with the leavings of the cut-up pages after what was wanted for the larger books had been chosen.

'The Reconstructed Carmelite Missal' now consists of three very large volumes measuring $28^1/_2$ by $22^1/_2$ inches. The great size of the original book, so inconvenient in a modern private library, may have contributed to its dismemberment. It is by no means, however, the largest book in the British Museum. One book, an antiphoner, is so big that it actually has wheels attached to the binding and is rolled rather than carried about. And just as young greenhorns, during their first days in a factory, are sent across to the stores to get a bucket of steam or some such damn fool errand, so neophyte librarians are handed orders for this book; after searching in vain for the non-existent reader they probably discover that the slip has been signed with the name A. Fool.

Among the many illuminations of the Carmelite Missal two are reproduced here. The initial T [figure 21 folio 68 verso] comes from the opening of the service dedicating a new church: *Terribilis est locus iste* – This is a fearsome place: it is the house of God, the gate of heaven. Before entering the church the bishop, preceded by a religious procession and followed by the wealthy lay patrons who have paid for the building, walks round the church three times, stopping at the main door on each circuit, knocking with his crozier and saying, '*Aperite portas principes vestras*'. In the miniature the bishop is sprinkling the church with holy water, an act which drives out the devil who is seen leaving in haste from the roof. Meanwhile Christ, detached from the worldly plane and placed in the margin, looks on benignly and gives the ceremony His blessing.

The other illustration [figure 17 folio 140] comes from the Exaltation of the Holy Cross, September 14: *Nos autem gloriari oportet in Cruce Domini nostri Jesu Christi:*

Incipiũt uespe de functorũ. a'. Placebo domino in regiõe uiuorũ. Ps.
Dilexi qm exaudiet dns: uocẽ orationis mee. Quia inclinauit aurẽ suã mihi: et in diebꝫ meis inuocabo.

24, 25 *(above and opposite)* Two details from a Franciscan Antiphoner produced in Italy *c.* 1444-50. Figure 24 depicts St Louis of Toulouse, a great-nephew of St Louis, King of France. Happy in his austere and humble life as a Franciscan, he was raised, much against his will, to be Archbishop of Toulouse. He died at the early age of twenty-three and, such was his reputation for sanctity, was almost immediately canonized. Figure 25 shows the opening initial B of the Psalms (*Beatus vir* etc.). The upper loop contains King David, while in the lower, St Francis himself, already bearing the stigmata, receives the three orders of Franciscans, who kneel at his feet

(It is for us to make our boast in the Cross of our Lord Jesus Christ). This lovely miniature gives a splendid display of fourteenth-century costume. The central figure, the Emperor Heraclius, was once thought to be a portrait of King Richard II surrounded by his knights, a claim which can no longer be upheld. It is always sad to abandon picturesque legends, but at least the shining armour and rich clothes give us a vivid picture of life at the court of that unfortunate king.

Whereas in the fourteenth century many scribes were kept busy producing Psalters, during the remaining years of the Middle Ages their patrons demanded illuminated copies of the *Horae* or Hours of the Virgin. This was not a church service book for priests, but a manual of private devotions for laymen, and, perhaps more often, laywomen. It contained a calendar of Saints' and Feast days, Gospel Lessons, certain Hours or services, the Penitential Psalms, prayers for the dead, etc.

Almost all of these books must have been produced in commercial workshops, the quality and scale of the illumination varying according to the purse of the patron. At the top of the scale these were royal and princely characters such as John, Duke of Bedford, brother of Henry V and Regent of France [figure 47], while humble examples were written for small merchants and craftsmen. The more splendid books were regarded as precious works of art rather than books to read and have generally survived in fine condition, but the lesser ones sometimes show great signs of use, like any other prayer book, and the great majority must have been read out of existence. The general run became somewhat stereotyped with six, twelve or twenty-four full-page miniatures, mostly of the same subjects, which in the more mediocre books were hackneyed copies of copies of copies. At the other end of the scale there are miniatures by some of the finest artists of the time, Van Eyck, Fouquet, Perugino and certain masters who, although they can be identified by their style, are unknown by name. A charming feature of *Horae* is the calendar, which contains a series of twelve small miniatures, the occupations of the months, that give a vivid insight into late medieval life. In the winter the lord and lady are generally sitting by the fire while Tom bears logs into the hall; in the spring they indulge in field sports, make music out of doors or go on pilgrimages, the sheep are shorn and later on the crops cut; then comes sowing and harrowing; lastly beasts are killed and salted down against the grim medieval winter [figures 26 & 51]. Very often the occupations of the month are accompanied by the signs of the zodiac which give considerable scope to a decorative artist. The calendar is of great use to the student in placing the origin of the manuscript. The major saints and the great feasts of the Church are, of course, universal; their days are entered in colour and give us the phrase 'red letter days'. But the presence of a group of minor Breton saints unknown outside north-west France, or the dedication of a church in Norwich must indicate that the book was written for a patron living in those parts. Certain differences in the liturgy – Use of Paris, Use of Sarum, Use of Sens, or Use of Tours, etc., are also a help in this direction.

The illustration taken from *The Bedford Book of Hours* [figure 47] shows the decorated page which faces the Memoria of St George. The Duke of Bedford, richly dressed in cloth of gold, kneels before St George, who wears the long blue mantle of the Garter. The margin contains five smaller pictures depicting the martyrdoms of St Andrew, patron of Burgundy, St Simon, St John the Evangelist, St Sigismund, King of Burgundy, who is being thrown into a well, and a nearly nude saint on horseback, who may be St Eric, King of Sweden. In the lower margin the Duke's arms are surrounded by his motto: *A vous entier*, (which also appears on a tapestry in the chapel).

Towards the end of the fifteenth century, chiefly in Paris, large quantities of *Horae* were printed on vellum, with engraved initials, borders and miniatures subsequently paint-

26 The life of a French noble family in winter is seen on this page of the calendar of a Book of Hours (fifteenth century). Pisces, the sign of the Zodiac, appears below

27 *(opposite)* Renaissance details, such as *putti*, fill this lavish border painted for the Medici Pope Leo X, son of Lorenzo the Magnificent

ed over by hand in opaque colours; to the casual eye these books must appear to be manuscripts.

Just as in the early days of gramophones and radio some superior persons scorned 'canned music', so Federigo da Montefeltro, Duke of Urbino (1422-82), refused to have a *printed* book in his library.

But the sands were running out. Imagine a scribe confronted with the first printed book; one man in a day could print more pages than a scribe could write in a year, and without danger of mistakes. The scribes' whole world had collapsed. By the mid-sixteenth century a few luxury manuscripts were produced as works of art or hieratic objects; some poor scholars actually made copies of printed books for their own use (as I remember students doing just after the last war when textbooks were virtually unobtainable). But henceforth almost all books were printed and the scribes and illuminators found that their livelihood had disappeared, just as, over the last hundred years, all kinds of handcrafts have gone down before the relentless advance of the machine.

Before turning to printing we must retrace our steps to fourteenth-century Italy, where the momentum of the medieval spirit was beginning to lose its force and the best spirits were turning for inspiration to the ancient world. This was the dawn of the Renaissance when Petrarch, 1304-74, and other poets and humanists were rediscovering the Greek and Latin classics which, during the later middle ages, stood forgotten on the monastic shelves. They eagerly copied these precious works for their own libraries. In doing so they would have dearly liked to write like 'the ancients', if only a single example of Roman handwriting had survived. They hated reading classical texts in what they had come to regard as a barbarous gothic script. To them 'gothic' was a term of contempt, and a later Italian linguist and poet, Giangiorgio Trissino, called his epic *L'Italia Liberata dai Goti*. So, they produced a new handwriting of their own. For the capitals they turned to Roman lapidary inscriptions of which a wealth of

28 A Renaissance manuscript of Lucretius, written in a humanist script and decorated with their favourite 'White-Vine' illumination

examples lay all around them, and derived their 'lower case' from the minuscule MSS of the school of Charlemagne. A superb example of this school may be seen in the British Museum, a copy of Lucretius bearing a colophon signed by the scribe Ioannes Rainaldus Mennius [figure 28]. This manuscript belonged in turn to Edward Poore (who lent it to Gilbert Wakefield), to the Marquis of Blandford (later Duke of Marlborough), Henry Drury (Master at Harrow and friend of Byron), P.A. Hanrott (who also owned the Carmelite Missal) and Bishop Butler. Another glorious example, also in the British Museum, is St Augustine, *De Civitate Dei*, [figure 52]. This was written at Naples during the later part of the fifteenth century for Inigo d'Avalos, Count of Monte Odorisio, Grand Chamberlain to Ferdinand of Aragon. It is interesting to note that this enthusiastic book-collector was appointed a Knight of the Garter by Edward IV. His arms appear in the lower part of a border which shows a typical mixture of pagan motifs, such as *putti*, with incidents from the life of St Augustine.

When the early printers turned their attention to the classics they cut types derived from the script in these manuscripts to satisfy the demand of the humanists. So that the 'roman' type which we read every day in the perfect form evolved by Mr Stanley Morison for *The Times* stems from Roman inscriptions, Charlemagne and the scholars of the Renaissance.

29 *(opposite)* St Clement I (reigned 89-97 AD), knew SS Peter and Paul personally; he was one of the earliest Popes. About 100 AD he was martyred by being thrown into the sea with an anchor tied to his neck, an event commemorated in this miniature from a manuscript produced for his namesake, Pope Clement VII. Clement VII (1523-34) was the son of Giuliano Medici (killed in the Pazzi conspiracy); he had the misfortune to catch the full force of the Reformation. It was he who excommunicated Henry VIII

LE
VII
A V
ON
AY
A
X

PARABOLE

Incipit prologus sancti iheronimi
presbiteri i parabolas salomonis
Iungat epistola quos iūgit sacerdoti-
um: immo carta non diuidat: quos
xpi nectit amor. Cōmētarios in osee-
amos ⁊ zachariā malachiā quoq;
poscitis. Scripsissē: si licuisset pre vali-
tudine. Mittitis solacia sumptuum.
notarios nr̄os et librarios sustenta-
tis: ut vobis potissimū nr̄m desudet
ingeniū. Et ecce ex latere frequēs turba
diuersa poscētiū: quasi aut equū sit me
vobis esurientibȝ aliis laborare: aut
in racione dati et accepti cuiq; preter
vos obnoxi⁹ sim. Itaq; lōga egrota-
tione fractus ne penitus hoc anno re-
ticerē ⁊ apud vos mutus essem: triduī
opus nomini vr̄o consecraui: interp̄-
tationē videlicet triū salomonis vo-
luminū: masloth qd̄ hebrei pabolas.
vulgata editio pūbia vocat: coeleth
quē grece ecclesiasten. latine cōcionatorē
possum⁹ dicere: sirasirim qd̄ ī linguā
nr̄am vertit̄ canticū cāticor. Fertur et
panaretos ihū filii sirach liber: ⁊ ali⁹
pseudographus qui sapientia salomonis inscribit̄. Quor priorē hebra-
icum reperi: nō ecclesiasticū ut apud la-
tinos: sed pabolas p̄notatū. Cui iūcti
erāt ecclesiastes et canticū canticor: ut
similitudinē salomonis nō solū nu-
mero librorū: sed etiā materiar gene-
re coequaret. Secūdus apud hebreos
nusq; est: quia et ipse stilus grecam
eloquētiā redolet: et nōnulli scriptor
veter hūc esse iudei filonis affirmāt.
Sicud ergo iudith ⁊ thobie ⁊ macha-
beor libros legit quidē eos ecclia: sed
inter canonicas scripturas nō recipit:
sic ⁊ hec duo volumina legat ad edi-
ficationē plebis: nō ad auctoritatem
ecclesiasticor dogmatū cōfirmandam.

Si cui sane septuaginta interpretum
magis editio placet: habet eā a nobis
olim emēdatā. Neq; enī noua sic cu-
dim⁹: ut vetera destruam⁹. Et tamē cū
diligētissime legerit: sciat magis nr̄a
scripta intelligi: que nō in terciū vas
trāsfusa coacuerit: sed statim de prelo
purissime cōmēdata teste: suū saporē ser-
vauerit. Incipiunt parabole salomonis

Parabole salomonis
filii dauid regis isrl̄:
ad sciendā sapienti-
am ⁊ disciplinā: ad
intelligenda verba
prudentie et suscipi-
endā erudicationē doctrine: iusticiā
et iudiciū ⁊ equitatē: ut detur paruulis
astucia: et adolescenti sciencia et intel-
lectus. Audiēs sapiēs sapiētior erit: ⁊
intelligēs gubernacula possidebit. Ani-
aduertet parabolam et interpretatio-
nem: verba sapientiū ⁊ enigmata eor.
Timor dn̄i principiū sapiētie. Sapien-
tiam atq; doctrinam stulti despiciūt.
Audi fili mi disciplinā pr̄is tui et ne
dimittas legem mr̄is tue: ut addatur
gracia capiti tuo: ⁊ torques collo tuo.
Fili mi si te lactauerint peccatores: ne ac-
quiescas eis. Si dixerit veni nobiscū.
insidiemur sāguini: abscōdam⁹ tedi-
culas cōtra insontem frustra: degluti-
amus eū sicud infernus viuentē ⁊ inte-
grum: quasi descēdentē in lacū: omnē
p̄ciosā sbstanciā reperiem⁹: implebim⁹
domus nr̄as spoliis: sortem mitte no-
biscum: marsupiū sit vnum omniū
nr̄m: fili mi ne ambules cū eis. Pro-
hibe pedem tuū a semitis eor. Pedes
enī illor ad malū currūt: ⁊ festināt ut
effundant sāguinem. Frustra autem
iacit̄ rete ante oculos pēnator. Ipsi q;
contra sanguinē suū insidiantur: et

CHAPTER TWO

Early Printing

NO INVENTION HAS ever had a greater influence on the development of mankind than that of printing. And in view of the fact that all those engaged in it must, of necessity, have been literate, it is surprising that no pioneer, no pious son, no favourite apprentice ever set down a contemporary account of what happened. This very paucity of information illustrates the difference which printing has made to knowledge. As it is, everything we know has been pieced together from minute fragments: records of lawsuits, parish or guild registers and intense examination of the books themselves. And when it is remembered that some of the most significant discoveries have been deduced from such minute evidence as the holes in the paper made by the pins which fixed it to the printing press, it will be realized to what extreme lengths scholarly thoroughness has pushed these studies. Even so, we are left with a jig-saw puzzle lacking half the pieces; but the following is, on the balance of probabilities, what we believe to have happened.

By the fifteenth century the number of people who could read and write had enormously increased. There was a crying need for some less laborious method of book production; and this was accentuated by the ground swell of two immense movements which, between them, did much to create modern Europe – the Renaissance and the Reformation. It has been said that in the Middle Ages men had more time than they had vellum, while during the Renaissance they had more paper than they had time.

31 A macabre Dance of Death from the *Nuremberg Chronicle* by Schedel, printed by Anton Koberger in 1493

30 *(opposite)* The *Gutenberg Bible*, the first book printed with movable types at Mainz, in 1455, with the illuminated decorations added by hand

The key to the whole invention was movable types, each piece consisting of a metal shaft with a letter of the alphabet in relief on the top. These may be set up in any desired order, to preach any desired message; mistakes can be corrected in proof; and after printing, the type is distributed and used again for another work or a later portion of the same book. Printing was the first form of mass production, virtually the only important one before the Industrial Revolution several hundred years later, where interchangeable parts are used to create unlimited quantities of identical objects.

There were immense difficulties in bringing this brilliant idea to a practical conclusion. The casting of the type must be so exact that the surface of the page is perfectly regular. Because of this many early printers were goldsmiths, i.e. men who were highly skilled at working to fine limits in metal. The second need was to produce some kind of ink which would readily transfer from metal to paper. The press was a simple transformation of the wine-press; paper had already been invented.

Johann Gutenberg, whom most of us honour as the inventor, was a man of patrician stock born at Mainz about 1398. He began his experiments at Strasbourg in the 1430s. These were very costly, and after moving to Mainz he borrowed money to finance them, in 1450, from a goldsmith and capitalist, Johann Fust. Having exhausted this in two years he obtained a further loan from the same source, giving, as security, a part interest in the new invention. In 1455 Fust brought a legal action to recover his money. Gutenberg was, of course, quite unable to pay, because any equity lay in the as yet unrealized fruits of his invention, so Fust impounded the equipment and remained in possession of the field. Some authorities postulate that Gutenberg was an impractical perfectionist who, so Fust thought, would continue with endless experiments and never actually produce a book. This view is too generous to Fust; most of us feel that it was a tragic and shameful situation in which Gutenberg was expelled from his own invention and deprived of the fruits of his genius.

Fust retained the services of Gutenberg's type-designer, Peter Schoeffer, who subsequently married his daughter and inherited the business. Schoeffer had begun life as a calligrapher; he now emerged as a brilliant typographer and technical printer. Whatever we may think about the means by which printing got into his hands, he did a great deal to advance it. Fust and Schoeffer printed, or at any rate completed, what is generally called '*The Gutenberg Bible*'. This called for very considerable organization and capital; six presses worked simultaneously, and many copies were printed on vellum. At this stage the title-page had not been invented, and the book bore no note which gave any clue to its origin, or even hinted that it was not a manuscript. There is a copy in the Bibliothèque Nationale, which was rubricated and bound by Heinrich Cremer, vicar of St Stephen's at Mainz, who signed and dated his work on its completion in August 1456. Allowing a few months for his task we may assume that the Bible came off the press in 1455 or, at the latest, towards the beginning of 1456. Work on it must have been well advanced before Gutenberg left the firm.

This, the first book to be printed, remains one of the most beautiful. The double columns of splendid gothic type embody centuries of development by generations of scribes and express the very core of the German medieval spirit. It is almost incredible that the first essay achieved such breath-taking perfection, as if printing, like Minerva, had sprung, fully armed, from the head of Zeus [figure 30].

In 1457 Fust and Schoeffer ascended to even greater heights. They produced a Psalter printed on vellum in black and red. In the Bible, as in the greater proportion of early printed books, the spaces for decorated initials were left blank, to be filled in later by rubricators like Heinrich Cremer. The 1457 Psalter contains elaborately decorated initials printed

32 The first printer's device of all was used by Fust and Schoeffer in Germany in 1462. A little above the twin shields which bear their arms, a hand-written note of ownership tells that this copy of St Augustine's *De Civitate Dei* originally belonged to the Monastery of the Blessed Virgin at Trier. It was presented by Louis, Duc de Bourbon, Bishop of Liège, in 1473

BEatus
vir ā Servite dn̄o. Evovae.
qui nō abijt in cōsilio impioꝝ: ⁊ in via peccatoꝝ nō
stetit: et in cathedra pestilē-
cie nō sedit. Sed in lege
dn̄i volūtas eius: ⁊ in lege ei⁹ meditabit̃ die
ac nocte. Et erit tanq̄ꝫ lignū qd̄ plantatū est
secus decursus aq̄rū: qd̄ fructū suū dabit in
tp̄e suo. Et foliū ei⁹ nō defluet: ⁊ oīa quecūqꝫ
faciet ꝓsperabunt̃. Non sic impij nō sic: sed
tanq̄ꝫ puluis quē proicit ventus a facie terre.
Ideo nō resurgūt impij in iudicio: neqꝫ pcc̄ō-
res in cōsilio iustoꝝ. Qm̄ nouit dn̄s viā iu-
storū: et iter impioꝝ ꝑibit. Gl̄a pri. Ps dd̄
Quare fremuerūt gētes: ⁊ pp̄li meditati
sūt inania. Astiterūt reges t̃re et principes ꝯuenerūt in vnū: adūsus dn̄m ⁊ adūsus
xp̄m ei⁹. Dirūpam⁹ vincla eoꝝ: ⁊ ꝓiciam⁹
a nobis iugū ipoꝝ. Qui habitat in celis irri-
debit eos: et dn̄s subsannabit eos. Tūc lo-
quet̃ ad eos in ira sua: et in furore suo cōtur-
babit eos. Ego aūt cōstitutus sū rex ab eo

in two colours, red and blue. The exactness of the register and the perfection of the technique is so consummate that until recently there was no agreement as to the method by which all this was achieved. In fact, as Sir Irvine Masson has now shown, the initials were constructed in two interlocking pieces, each of which was separately inked in colour, reassembled, and then printed together with the page of text at a single pull of the press [figure 33]. The Psalter was also the first book to contain a colophon declaring where, when and by whom it had been printed. Ten copies have survived, of which the most perfect (known as the 'virgin' copy) was never used for church services and is preserved in Vienna. Should this ever, through some revolution, come on to the open market it would probably prove to be the most valuable printed book in the world.

Meanwhile poor Gutenberg was apparently left in possession of some equipment, perhaps that which had not been paid for with Fust's money. It was probably Gutenberg himself who, in 1457, printed a Bible, generally known as the Thirty-six-Line Bible to distinguish it from the forty-two lines of its precursor, and three years later used a new small type for a large Latin dictionary, Joannes Balbus's *Catholicon*, the first large secular book. But without Fust's business connections and practical acumen Gutenberg did not succeed. The Thirty-six-Line Bible has survived in only nine copies, (as against forty-seven of its rival), the *Catholicon* was remaindered by Fust and Schoeffer and its type passed into other hands. Gutenberg became a pensioner of the Archbishop of Mainz and died in 1468 [figure 34].

Meanwhile printing spread like wildfire. Journeymen left their masters and set up by themselves in other towns or countries, the dispersal being accentuated when, in 1462, Mainz was sacked by one of its rival archbishops.

Two German printers, Conrad Sweynheym and Arnold Pannartz, proceeded to Italy, the centre of the Church and the

34 The Thirty-six-Line Bible, Mainz, 1457, was probably printed by Gutenberg after he had been deprived of the major equipment of his own invention

33 *(opposite)* The decorated initial 'B' shown in colour (figure 56) as it appears set in proportion on the full page of Fust and Schoeffer's *Psalter*

OGITANTI MIHI SEPENVME-
ro & memoria uetera repetenti perbea-
ti fuisse. Q. frater illi uideri solent qui in
optima. RE. PV: quom & honoribus &
reꝝ gestarū gloria florerent eū uitę cur-
sum tenere potuerūt: ut uel ī negotio sine
periculo: uel in ocio cū dignitate esse possent: At nunc quod
mihi quoqꝫ initiū requiescēdi atqꝫ animū adutriusqꝫ nostꝝ
pręclara studia referendi fore iustum et prope ab omnibus
cōcessum arbitrarer: si infinitus forensiū reꝝ labor: et am-
bitionis occupatio de cursu honoꝝ etiā ętatis flexu cōstitisset
quā spem cogitationū & consilioꝝ meoꝝ cū graues cōueni-
entiū tēpoꝝ: tum uarii nr̄i casus fefellerunt: Nam qui locus
quietis & trāquillitatis plenissimus fore uidebat̄: ī eo maxime moles molestiaꝝ & turbulētissime tēpestates: extiterīt:
Neqꝫ uero nobis cupientibus atqꝫ exoptātibus fructus ocii
datus est: ad eas artis quibus a pueris dediti fuimus cele-
brādas inter nosqꝫ recolendas: Nam ꝑma ętate incidimus
in ipam ꝑturbationē disciplinę ueteris: & cōsulatū deueni-
mus ī mediū reꝝ omniū certamē atqꝫ discrimen: & hoc tp̄s
omne post cōsulatū obiecimus his fluctibus: qui ꝑ nos a cō-
muni peste depulsi in nos metipos redundarēt: Sed tamen
ī eis uel asperitatibus reꝝ uel angustiis temporis obsequar
studiis nostris: & q̄tum mihi uel fraus iimicorum uel causa
amicoꝝ: uel res. p. tribuet otii ad scribendū potissimū con-
ferā: Tibi uero frater neqꝫ hortanti deero neqꝫ rogāti: nā
neqꝫ auctoritate quisq̄ apud me plus ualere te potest: neqꝫ

35 This edition of the Orations of Cicero, printed in the monastery at Subiaco near Rome in 1465 by Sweynheym and Pannartz, is the earliest surviving book to have been printed in Italy

36 *(opposite)* The first printed edition of Euclid's *Elements of Geometry*, Venice, 1482, was embellished with borders and initials which made even a textbook an object of beauty. This was the work of Erhard Ratdolt, whose style later greatly influenced William Morris

home of humanism. Naturally enough they had intended to start in Rome, but before they got there they found a patron in Cardinal Turrecremata, the Abbot of Subiaco.

Subiaco, the birthplace of Benedictine monasticism, is romantically situated among the mountains already hallowed by the little farm which Maecenas gave to Horace. It is a monastery with strong scholarly traditions, and in the mid-fifteenth century contained many German monks. Here Sweynheym and Pannartz, beginning in 1465, produced three books in an attractive type [figure 35]; they probably regarded this as roman, but it contains a certain element of gothic which gives it individuality and vigour; and in our own time St John Hornby revived this type for his Ashendene Press. Two years later, in 1467, they moved on to Rome and set up shop in the Massimi Palace. Here, printing in a genuine but rather untidy roman type, they specialized in the works of the major Christian Fathers and the classics of the ancient world in large stately folios of the kind 'without which no monastic (or cardinal's) library is complete'.

It might have been expected that Rome, the city to which pilgrims came from all over the western world, would become the home of Italian printing. But a major problem for the early printers was the distribution of their books. The most important centres of printing are therefore to be found in the great trading cities, and above all Venice. The Venetians had worked out banking systems, double-entry book-keeping and the technique of commerce at a time when most Britons were still living in mud huts. They had depots and agents everywhere and Venetian galleys made their way to all parts of the known world. Venice in the fifteenth century was not unlike England in her greater days – governed by an oligarchy, with traditions of independence and a comparative freedom from the Inquisition which favoured the expression of thought. Here printing first really developed as a business, and about one hundred and fifty presses had been founded in the city by 1500. The

Preclarissimus liber elementorum Euclidis perspi-
cacissimi: in artem Geometrie incipit quã foelicissime:

Punctus est cuius ps nõ est. ¶ Linea est
lõgitudo sine latitudine cui⁹ quidẽ extremitates sũt duo pũcta. ¶ Linea recta
ẽ ab vno pũcto ad aliũ breuissima extẽsio i extremitates suas vtrũqʒ eoꝝ reci
piens. ¶ Supficies ẽ q̃ lõgitudinẽ ⁊ lati
tudinẽ tm̃ hʒ: cui⁹ termi quidẽ sũt linee.
¶ Supficies plana ẽ ab vna linea ad a-
liã extẽsio i extremitates suas recipiẽs
¶ Angulus planus ẽ duarũ linearũ al-
ternus ꝯtactus: quaꝝ expãsio ẽ sup sup-
ficiẽ applicatioqʒ nõ directa. ¶ Quãdo aũt angulum ꝯtinẽt due
linee recte rectiline⁹ angulus noiat. ¶ Qñ recta linea sup rectã
steterit duoqʒ anguli vtrobiqʒ fuerit eq̃les: eoꝝ vterqʒ rect⁹ erit
¶ Lineaqʒ linee supstãs ei cui supstat ppendicularis vocat. ¶ An
gulus vo qui recto maior ẽ obtusus dicit. ¶ Angul⁹ vo minor re
cto acut⁹ appellat. ¶ Termin⁹ ẽ qd vniuscuiusqʒ finis ẽ. ¶ Figura
ẽ q̃ tmino vl termis ꝯtinet. ¶ Circul⁹ ẽ figura plana vna q̃dem linea ꝯtẽta: q̃ circũferentia noiat: in cui⁹ medio pũct⁹ ẽ: a quo oẽs
linee recte ad circũferẽtiã exeũtes sibiinuicẽ sũt equales. Et hic
quidẽ pũct⁹ cẽtrũ circuli dr. ¶ Diameter circuli ẽ linea recta que
sup ei⁹ centꝝ trãsiens extremitatesqʒ suas circũferẽtie applicans
circulũ i duo media diuidit. ¶ Semicirculus ẽ figura plana dia-
metro circuli ⁊ medietate circũferentie ꝯtenta. ¶ Portio circuli ẽ figura plana recta linea ⁊ parte circũferẽtie ꝯtẽta: semicircu-
lo quidẽ aut maior aut minor. ¶ Rectilinee figure sũt q̃ rectis lineis cõtinent quarũ quedã trilatere q̃ trib⁹ rectis lineis: quedã
quadrilatere q̃ q̃tuor rectis lineis. q̃dã mltilatere que pluribus
q̃ʒ quatuor rectis lineis continent. ¶ Figurarũ trilaterarũ: alia
est triangulus hñs tria latera equalia. Alia triangulus duo hñs
eq̃lia latera. Alia triangulus triũ inequalium laterũ. Haꝝ iterũ
alia est orthogoniũ: vnũ .s. rectum angulum habens. Alia ẽ am-
bligonium aliquem obtusum angulum habens. Alia est oxigoni
um: in qua tres anguli sunt acuti. ¶ Figurarũ autẽ quadrilateraꝝ
Alia est q̃dratum quod est equilaterũ atqʒ rectangulũ. Alia est
tetragon⁹ long⁹: q̃ est figura rectangula: sed equilatera non est.
Alia est helmuaym: que est equilatera: sed rectangula non est.

De principijs p se notis: ⁊ pmo de diffini
tionibus earundem.

37 Aldus Manutius, the greatest scholar-printer, was the first to publish 'pocket editions' of the great classics. This Catullus, printed in Venice in 1515, the year of his death, is shown slightly reduced from its actual size of 6¾ x 4¼ ins, in its contemporary Venetian binding of black morocco

38 *(opposite left)* This *Natural History* of Pliny was printed by Jenson in Venice in 1472, in type which is often considered the most beautiful ever designed, and which has had the most effect on the modern revival of fine printing

first men to work in Venice were John and Wendelin of Speier who set up in 1469, and, in order to satisfy the demands of the humanists, produced the first really satisfactory roman type. But the most important for our purpose were two printers of genius: Jenson and Aldus.

Nicolaus Jenson, a Frenchman born near Troyes, is the first really important printer who was not a German. As Master of the Royal Mint (once again the connection with metalwork) he was sent to Mainz in secret by his king to spy out the new invention of printing. That was in 1458, after which we lose sight of him until he set up on his own in Venice in 1470. Although Jenson's was not the first humanist type it is by far the best. Each letter is beautiful in itself, but not too perfect (absolute perfection sometimes results in deadness), and, what is far more important and difficult to achieve, the letters combine well together into an harmonious whole. This type has been the admiration of printers ever since, and those who have sought to revive printing in later days have often turned to it for inspiration. It is to be found in a considerable number of books, but by general consensus the *Pliny* of 1472 is regarded as Jenson's masterpiece. It is hard to believe that such perfection was a prentice effort; in the twelve years between 1458 and 1470 Jenson may have designed types for others, but of these dark years we know nothing [figure 38].

Jenson was primarily a craftsman of genius. The approach to printing of Aldus Manutius was quite different; he was a scholar with a passion for the ancient classics consumed by a desire to produce accurate texts and put them into as many hands as possible. Born in 1450, he spent his early life as tutor to the sons of the Prince of Carpi and so fired them with his own enthusiasm that the elder of his pupils later put up the money to found the Aldine press. There was no rush to get into print. In 1490 an academy of scholars was founded in Venice, manuscripts were collected and collated, the best possible texts were prepared. The first books came out in

CAII PLYNII SECVNDI NATVRALIS HISTORIAE LIBER .I.

CAIVS PLYNIVS SECVNDVS NOVOCOMENSIS DOMITIANO SVO SALVTEM. PRAEFATIO.

IBROS NATVRALIS HISTORIAE NO‑
uitium camœnis quiritium tuorum opus natum
apud me proxima fœtura licentiore epiſtola nar‑
rare conſtitui tibi iucundiſſime imperator. Sit.n.
hæc tui præfatio ueriſſima: dum maxio cōſeneſcit
in patre. Nāq; tu ſolebas putare eſſe aliqd meas
nugas: ut obiicere moliar Catullum conterraneū
meum. Agnoſcis & hoc caſtrēſe uerbum. Ille enī
ut ſcis: permutatis prioribus ſyllabis duriuſculū
ſe fecit: q̄ uolebat exiſtimari a uernaculis tuis: &
famulis. Simul ut hac mea petulātia fiat: quod
proxime nō fieri queſtus es: i alia procaci epiſto‑
la noſtra: ut in quædam acta exeāt. Sciantq; omnes: q̄ ex æquo tecum uiuat impium.
Triumphalis & cenſorius tu ſextumque conſul ac tribunicia potestatis particeps. Et
quod iis nobilius feciſti: dū illud patri pariter & equeſtri ordini præſtas præfectus præ‑
torii eius: omniaq; hæc reipub. Et nobis quidem qualis in caſtrēſi contubernio? Nec
quicq̄ mutauit in te fortunæ amplitudo in iis: niſi ut prodeſſe tantundem poſſes: &
uelles. Itaq; cum cæteris in ueneratione tui pateant omnia illa: nobis ad colendum te
familiarius audacia ſola ſupereſt. Hanc igitur tibi imputabis: & in noſtra culpa tibi
ignoſces. Perfricui faciem: nec tamen profeci. Quando alia uia occurris ingens. Et
longius etiam ſubmoues ingenii facibus. Fulgurat in nullo unq̄ uerius dicta uis elo‑
quentiæ. Tibi tribunitiæ poteſtatis facūdia. Quāto tu ore patris laudes tonas? Quā‑
to fratris amas? Quantus in poetica es? O magna fœcunditas animi. Quēadmodū
fratrem quoq; imitareris: excogitaſti. Sed hæc quis poſſet intrepidus æſtimare? ſubi‑
turus ingenii tui iudicium: præſertim laceſſitum? Neque enim ſimilis eſt conditio
publicantium: & nominatim tibi dicantium. Tum poſſem dicere: quid iſta legis im‑
perator? Humili uulgo ſcripta ſunt: agricolarum: opificum turbæ: deniq; ſtudiorū
ocioſis. Quid te iudicem facis? Cum hanc operam condicerem: non eras in hoc albo.
Maiorem te ſciebam: q̄ ut deſcenſurum huc putarem. Præterea eſt quædam publica ‑
etiam eruditorum reiectio. Vtitur illa & .M. Tullius extra omnem ingenii aleam po‑
ſitus. Et quod miremur: per aduocatum defēditur. Hæc doctiſſimum omniū Perſiū
legere nolo. Lælium Decimum uolo. Quod ſi hoc Lucillius qui primus cōdidit ſtili
naſum: dicēdum ſibi putauit. Si Cicero mutuandū: præſertim cum de repub. ſcribe‑

1494. By that time many of the Latin classics were already in print, so that the majority of Aldus's first books were in Greek. In the course of his career Aldus printed the first Greek editions of Aristophanes, Aristotle, and then, from 1502 onwards, of Aeschylus, Sophocles, Plato, Demosthenes, Herodotus and Pindar. No other publisher has ever made such a staggering contribution to the human spirit. The first half of his ambition had been nobly achieved. But these books, like the great majority of contemporary publications, were large and expensive to buy. Aldus next revolutionized publishing itself: he produced the pocket edition. In place of the stately folios fit for the library of a cardinal he printed small books, half a dozen of which would pack into the saddle-bag of a wandering scholar. In order to do this he

39 'Italics' made their first printed appearance as the tiny letters on the pages of the book held by St Catherine of Siena in a woodcut portrait from her *Epistole Devotissime* in an edition by Aldus, Venice, 1500

40, 41 *(overleaf)* Before the invention of movable types, a few rudimentary books were produced in which text and illustrations were cut on the same block of wood. The *Biblia Pauperum* consists of parallel incidents in the Old and New Testaments, from which moral lessons could be drawn

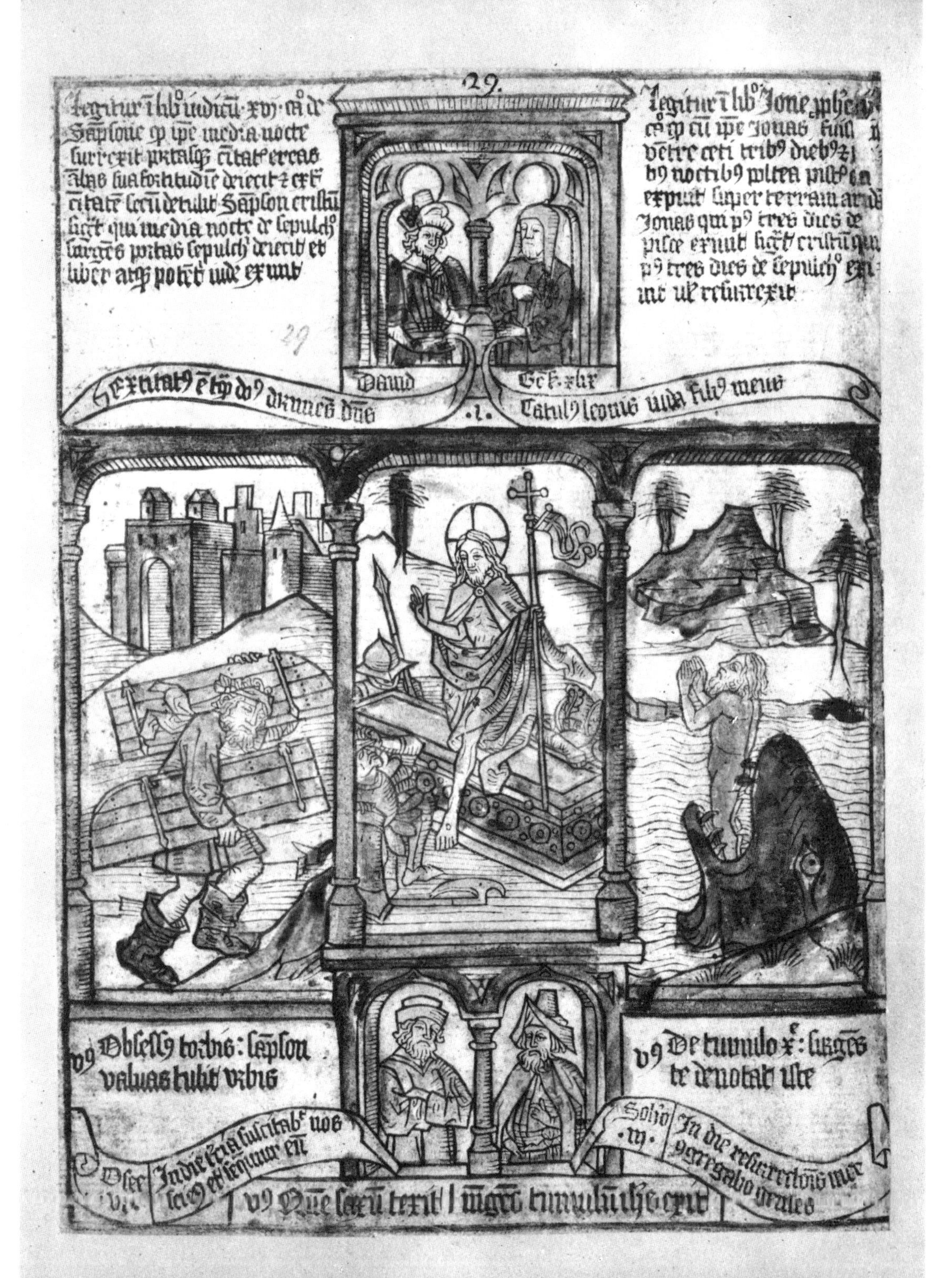
29.
David

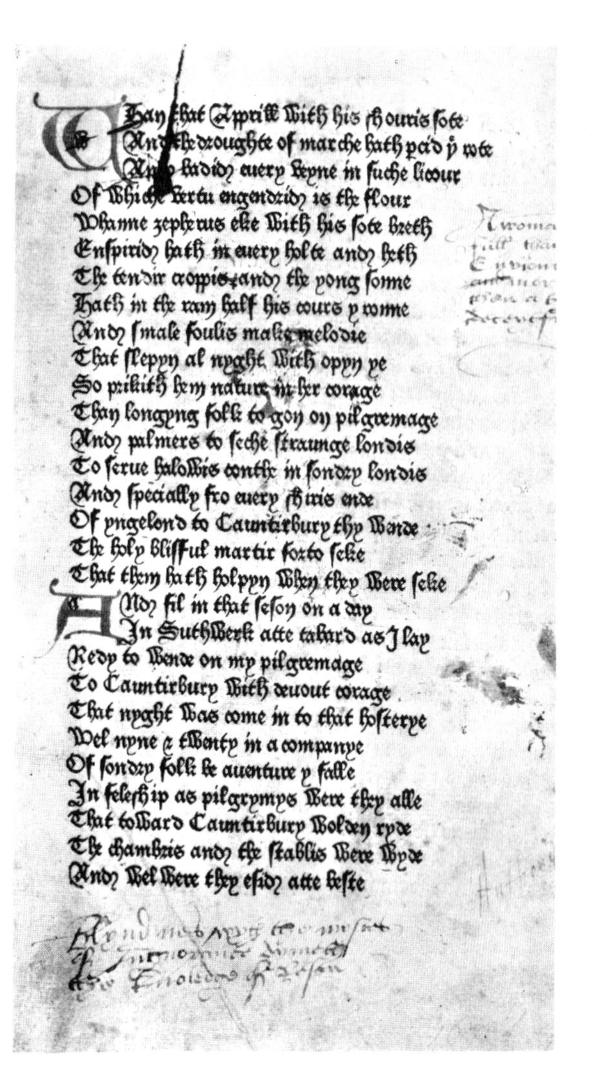

Whan that Apprill with his shouris sote
And the droughte of marche hath percid y rote
And badid every veyne in suche licour
Of which vertu engendrid is the flour
Whanne zepherus eke with his sote breth
Enspirid hath in every holte and heth
The tendir croppis and the yong sonne
Hath in the ram half his cours y ronne
And smale foulis make melodie
That slepyn al nyght with opyn ye
So prikith hem nature in her corage
Than longyng folk to goon on pilgremage
And palmers to seche straunge londis
To serue halowis couthe in sondry londis
And specially fro every shiris ende
Of yngelond to Cauntirbury they wende
The holy blisful martir forto seke
That them hath holpyn whan they were seke
And fil in that seson on a day
In Suthwerk atte tabard as I lay
Redy to wende on my pilgremage
To Cauntirbury with devout corage
That nyght was come in to that hostelrye
Wel nyne & twenty in a companye
Of sondry folk be aventure y falle
In feleship as pilgrymys were they alle
That toward Cauntirbury wolden ryde
The chambris and the stablis were wyde
And wel were they esid atte beste

42 The opening of Chaucer's *Canterbury Tales*, printed in Westminster by William Caxton in 1478

commissioned an entirely new type, an italic based on the chancery hand used by the Vatican scribes. The first small book in the new type was the Virgil of 1501 and this was followed by a high proportion of the classics.

William Caxton, the first English printer, born in Kent about 1422, spent a great part of his life at Bruges working as a merchant and 'governor of the English colony', a kind of consul. He was one of that sympathetic type, the sensitive man of affairs who devotes his leisure to literature; akin to Chaucer, who for the greater part of his life worked as a civil servant. Encouraged by his patron, Margaret of Burgundy, sister of Edward the Fourth, Caxton translated Raoul le Fèvre's *Recuyell of the Hystoryes of Troye*. The picture of Troy which filled the minds of le Fèvre and Caxton was probably not unlike Bruges itself, a medieval walled city, with belfries and red tiled roofs. William Morris, who reprinted this work at the Kelmscott Press, wrote: 'It makes a thoroughly amusing story, instinct with medieval thought and manners. For, though written at the end of the Middle Ages and dealing with classical mythology, it has in it no token of the coming Renaissance, but is purely medieval. It is the last issue of that story of Troy which through the whole of the Middle Ages had such a hold on men's imaginations; the story built up from a rumour of the Cyclic Poets, of the heroic city of Troy, defended by Priam and his gallant sons, led by Hector the *Preux Chevalier*, and beset by the violent and brutal Greeks, who were looked on as the necessary machinery for bringing about the undeniable tragedy of the fall of the city.' Caxton's translation was a great success among the English colony and his friends clamoured for copies. 'And for as moche as in the wrytyng of the same my penne is worn,' he says, 'myn hand wery and not stedfast, myn eyen dimmed with overmoche lokyng on the whit paper . . .' There was only one way out of this impasse, a rather desperate one: he went to Cologne and learned how to print. On returning to Bruges he set up his own press, starting with

The Hystoryes of Troye, 1474, the first book to be printed in English. In the autumn of 1476 he crossed into England, rented premises in Westminster and set up his press; in 1477 he printed *The Dictes or Sayengis of the Philosophers.*

Caxton was one of the first men other than a German to introduce printing into a new country. It must be admitted that his technical abilities were not so high nor his types so beautiful as those of his continental confrères; his interests and abilities lay in another direction. Nearly all the other first printers were craftsmen primarily interested in printing itself, or businessmen interested in making money. Caxton was a man of letters who would be remembered for his services to English literature even if he had never printed at all. Of the hundred-and-three editions known to have been printed by him twenty were in his own translations, while many others contain prefaces in his vivid and racy style; he printed the first editions of Lydgate, Malory and Chaucer [figure 42].

In the early days of printing the title-page had not been invented; information regarding the name of the printer, the place of printing and other data was given in the colophon, a final paragraph which is generally found at the end of the text or the end of the book. In 1462 Fust and Schoeffer began to sign their work regularly with a woodcut printer's device. It consisted of two shields with their respective coats of arms hanging from a bough printed near the colophon [figure 32]. This was a development of the medieval merchant's mark with which other craftsmen had long put a seal on their own work. Many printers followed suit and the resulting wealth of woodcut designs forms an attractive feature of early printing.

Aldus, too, had his printer's device, which is perhaps the most famous of them all. It was based on a coin of the Roman emperor Titus, given to him by Cardinal Bembo; the dolphin and anchor symbolize Aldus's motto: Hasten Slowly. Figure 44 shows an early state of this device in which the border, found in the first state, has been almost entirely cut away, leaving a series of dots. Caxton's device [figure 43] consists

43 William Caxton's bold initials sufficed to sign the first books printed in England

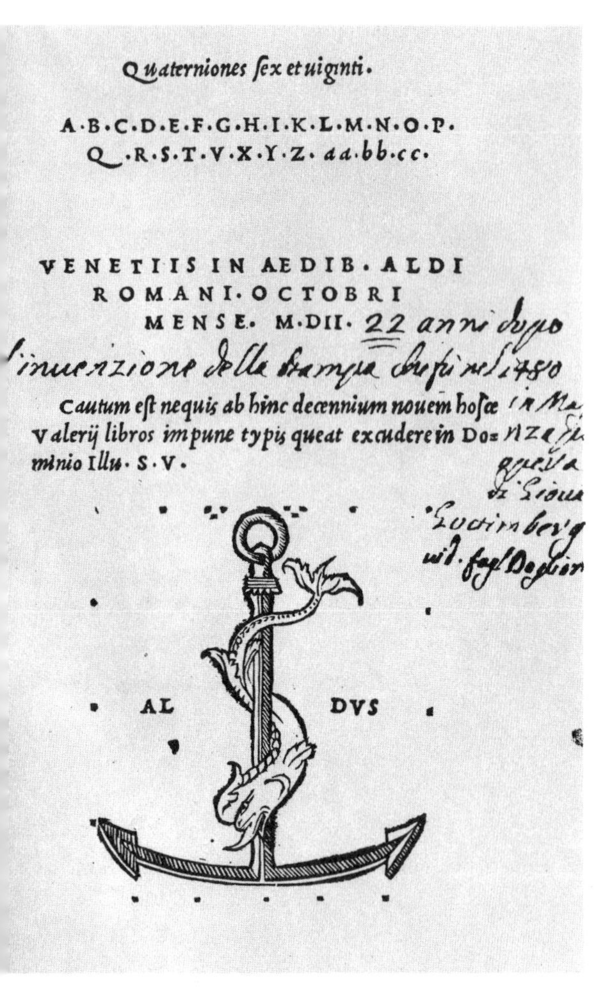
Quaterniones sex et uiginti.

A·B·C·D·E·F·G·H·I·K·L·M·N·O·P·
Q·R·S·T·V·X·Y·Z· aa·bb·cc·

VENETIIS IN AEDIB· ALDI
ROMANI· OCTOBRI
MENSE· M·DII·

Cautum est nequis ab hinc decennium nouem hosce
Valerij libros impune typis queat excudere in Do=
minio Illu· S·V·

AL DVS

44 Perhaps the most famous device is that of the Venetian, Aldus, whose Dolphin and Anchor appear on this page of Valerius Maximus, 1502

of his initials surrounded by a little elementary decoration.

The printing of individual woodblocks preceded the production of books by means of movable types. Textile printing had been established in Egypt by the sixth century AD, while the Chinese carried on all kinds of block printing a good deal earlier. In addition to the decoration of textiles European craftsmen produced individual pictures and playing cards during the fourteenth century. There are references to playing card manufacture in the German cities of Ulm and Augsburg, which afterwards became famous for book illustration, while in 1430 a Florentine artist, filling in his income tax returns, mentions the woodblocks from which he printed playing cards. St Bernardino, like Savonarola half a century later, moved great crowds to emotional repentance by the power of his sermons. His Lenten preaching at Bologna in 1424 had such effect that all who heard it burned their playing cards (which was less to be deplored than the exhortations of Savonarola that drove his congregations into burning paintings by Botticelli), whereupon a card-maker who faced ruin came to St Bernardino with his troubles and the saint advised him to manufacture sacred pictures instead.

During the fourteenth century there had been a great increase in pilgrimages; woodcut pictures of the saints were on sale at favoured shrines, and no doubt Chaucer's Wife of Bath collected quite a batch during her peregrinations.

One of the finest woodcut portraits of a saint, and the first to bear a date, 1423, depicts St Christopher carrying the Christ child across a river. Only one example has survived, pasted into a manuscript, written in 1417, which was once in the Charterhouse at Buxheim and is now preserved in the John Rylands Library, Manchester. As will be seen [figure 45] this woodcut has two lines of text.

It was an obvious step from printing single pages with a little text to the production of rudimentary books in which each page, containing both text and illustrations, was printed from a single woodblock. A handful of these early block-books have survived, the dating of which has been a matter for more or less scholarly conjecture and discussion since the history of printing first became an object of study, and many learned monographs and essays have been written with varying conclusions. But the problem has recently been solved, beyond doubt, by Allan Stevenson, who has shown, by accurately dating the paper used in block-books, that the first edition of the earliest of these, the *Apocalypse*, appeared towards 1451 (a little before the Gutenbergian *Indulgences* of 1454 which are the earliest known type-printed pieces), while the earliest editions of the *Biblia Pauperum* and *Ars Moriendi* were produced towards 1462 and 1466 respectively.

The public at whom the block-books were aimed is sufficiently shown by the title later invented for one of them: *Biblia Pauperum (The Bible of the Poor)*. In this book parallel incidents from the Old and New Testaments are placed side by side in order to illustrate spiritual truths. Thus in figure 41 the Resurrection is placed between Jonah emerging from the whale and Samson carrying off the gates of Gaza: men whom God wanted to be saved; strong men breaking out from disaster. The caption under Samson reads:

Obsessus turbis Sampson
Valvas tulit urbis.

Samson, oppressed by the crowd, carries off the gates of the city; a Leonine hexameter with internal rhymes. This form of versifying calls for a degree of ingenuity (hardly justified by the generally ugly results) which is only equalled by the tortuous parallels of medieval sermonizing. In figure 40 the Crucifixion is flanked by the creation of Eve and Moses striking the rock and causing living water to spring forth: all examples of the creation of life, here and hereafter. Or, to take the analogies further: when Longinus pierced the side of Christ with his spear blood and water flowed forth; even so Moses caused living water to flow by a blow from his rod and God the Father drew Eve out of Adam's side. Village priests and others whose imagination and education

45 St Christopher bears the Christ-child safely across a river in the earliest woodcut portrait of a saint to be dated, 1423. This, the only surviving example, is in the John Rylands Library in Manchester

46 The *Ars Moriendi*, the *Art of Dying*, celebrates the triumph of the Christian at the moment of death; it is one of the block-books produced in the fifteenth century

47 *(opposite)* A Book of Hours, written early in the fifteenth century for John, Duke of Bedford, who is seen kneeling before Saint George

were inadequate to the writing of their own sermons could make an edifiying use of this book, and in many cases illustrate their discourse from the murals which in those days were to be seen painted on the walls of parish churches. Another important block-book was the *Ars Moriendi*, the *Art of Dying*, the human soul faced with 'the undiscover'd country from whose bourn no traveller returns'. Dr Henry Guppy, the very distinguished librarian of the John Rylands Library, Manchester, described this book:

> The object of the book is to describe the temptations that beset the dying. The first picture represents the dying man as tempted by devils concerning his faith. The succeeding picture shows the good angels who enable him to remain steadfast. In like manner the dying man is tempted by devils to despair, to impatience and to avarice, but through the help of angels he triumphs over all his adversaries. In the last of the series the spirit of the dying man is being exhaled from his mouth, and is received by the angels, to the utter disgust of the baffled devils who display frightful contortions as they beat a retreat.

There are certain parallels between block-books and the strip cartoons which, in our own time, appear in the more popular newspapers; both develop their story in a series of related pictures, in both the speech of the characters is contained in 'balloons'. In figure 46 the angel says 'Be firm in thy faith'; the defeated devils, in their rage, cry 'Let us flee', 'We are conquered' and 'We labour in vain'. Both are produced for the semi-literate; the block-books for those who were given no chance in life, the strip cartoons for those who, in spite of the hundreds of millions poured out on education, retain their intellectual sow's-eardom. Only the motives of the producers and the nature of the message have changed – from Gethsemane to Gadarene swine.

Although the craft of cutting woodblocks had preceded the invention of printing, the earliest incunabula were not illustrated, the first printers having enough technical problems on their hands as it was. When Albrecht Pfister of Bamberg produced the first illustrated book, *Der Ackermann*

Adam et Eua eiecti sunt de paradiso. Genesis tercio Capitulo. Adam vnd Eua seyent außgeworffen von dem paradeiß.

Nec a mortis potestate sufficienter defensare. In extre
ma necessitate nullum prestat homini iuuamen. Sed
tribuit corpi vilissimum lintheamen. Mundus ergo
iste videtur recte esse tanquam sambucus. Cuius flos
est pulcher. sed amarus eius fructus. Sic pulchra vi
det mundi delectatio. Et fructus eius est eterna dam
natio. Mundus etiam iude traditori conuenienter
comparatur. Per quam xpus osculo doloso tradebatur
Tale signum mundus dat demonibus. Quale iudas
dedit ihu xpi hostibus. Quem osculatus fuero diuiti-
as et honores dando. Ipse est tenete eum eternaliter
cruciando. Veruntamen diuitie non semper sunt ad
damnationem. Sed multis prosunt ad eternam sal
uationem. Dixit enim Daniel Nabuchodonosor re-
gi. Peccata tua elemosinis redime. viam salutis das
ei. Deus enim potentes non abicit. cum sit ipse po
tens. Si vtuntur temporalibus sicut Thobias dixit. filiu suu docens. Si multu tibi fuerit habundanter
tribue. Si modicu tibi fuit. idipm libenter impartire stude.

48, 49, 50 The cities of Augsburg and Ulm were famous for the production of beautiful woodcuts in the Gothic style. These three from the *Speculum Humanae Salvationis*, Augsburg, about 1473, show great sympathy between the design of the woodcuts and the type

von Böhmen, about 1460, he did not attempt both processes simultaneously but printed the text first and left spaces for the woodcuts. We know this because the only surviving copy in the library at Wolfenbüttel lacks the woodcuts which appear in the second edition. In most cases the early books have simple outline cuts which were intended to be coloured by hand. The early printers left spaces in which rubricators were expected to paint illuminated initials, though in a majority of cases these spaces remain blank; but a much higher proportion of the first woodcuts are coloured, leading us to suppose that the colouring was done in the printing shop.

After the handful of books printed by Pfister between 1460 and 1464 there is a gap of several years before the next illustrated book (the *Turrecremata* of 1467 printed at Rome by Ulrich Han) was undertaken. It might have been thought that so attractive a product would meet with immediate success and wide emulation, but the problems were not only technical. When Günther Zainer attempted work of a like kind at Augsburg he immediately ran into the organized opposition of the guilds, whose selfish and purblind obstruction resembled the chalk-line and demarcation trade union disputes of our own day. It was only through the intelligent and powerful intervention of Melchior von Stamhaim, the Abbot of SS Ulrich and Afra, that a working compromise

51 *(overleaf left)* Spring is greeted with music-making on this page from a fifteenth-century French Book of Hours; the season is indicated by a sign of the Zodiac

52 *(overleaf right)* The opening page of a Renaissance manuscript of St Augustine, *De Civitate Dei*, written in Naples in the fifteenth century for the Count of Monte Odorisio. Pagan motifs mingled in the elaborate decoration surround scenes from the life of the saint

xii	e		xx
i	f		xxi
iii	g	Inuentio dionysii &	xxii
ix	A	Georgii martiris	xxiii
	b		xxiiii
xvii	c	Marci euangeliste	xxv
vi	d	Cleti pape & martiris	xxvi
	e		xxvii
xiiii	f	Vitalis martiris	xxviii
iii	g	Petri martiris	xxix
	A	Eutropii epi & martiris	xxx

AVRELII AVGVSTINI DOCTOR[illegible] EXIMII DE CIVITATE DEI LIBER PRIMVS FELICITER [illegible]CIPIT.

LORIOSISSIMAM CIVITATEM DEI
SIVE IN HOC TEMPORVM CVRSV CVM
inter impios peregrinatur ex fide uiuens siue
in illa stabilitate sedis aeternae quam nunc expe
ctat per patientiam quoad usq. iustitia conuerta
tur in iudicium deinceps adeptura per excellentia
uictoriam ultimam et pacem perfectam hoc opere
ad te instituto et mea ad te promissione debito de
fendere aduersus eos qui conditori eius deos suos p̄
ferunt fili carissime marcelline suscepi. Magnum
opus et arduum. sed deus adiutor noster est. Nam scio quibus uiribus opus sit
ut persuadeatur superbis quanta sit uirtus humilitatis qua fit ut omnia terre
na cacumina temporali mobilitate nutantia non humano usurpata fastu sed
diuina gratia donata celsitudo transcendat. Rex enim et conditor ciuitatis hu
ius de qua loqui instituimus in scriptura populi sui sententiam diuine legis ape
ruit qua dictum est. Deus superbis resistit. humilibus aūt dat gratiam. Hoc ue
ro quod dei est superbe quoq. anime spiritus inflatus affectat amatq. sibi in lau
dibus dici: Parcere subiectis et debellare superbos. Vnde etiam de ciuitate terre
na quae cum dominari appetit et si populi seruiant ipsa ei dominandi libido do
minatur non est pretereundum silentio quicquid dicere suscepti huius operis ra
tio postulat et facultas datur. Ex hac namq. existunt inimici aduersus quos de
fendenda est dei ciuitas quorum tamen multi correcto impietatis errore ciues in ea fiut
satis idonei. multi uero in eam tantis exardescunt ignibus odiorum. tamq. mani
festis beneficiis redemptoris eius ingrati sunt ut hodie contra eam linguas non
mouerent nisi ferrum hostile fugientes in sacratis eius locis uitam de qua super
biunt inuenirent. An non etiam illi romani christi nomini infesti sunt. quibus
propter xp̄m barbari pepercerunt? Testantur hec martyrum loca et basilicae apo
stolorum. que in illa uastatione urbis ad se confugientes suos alienosq. receperut.
Hucusq. cruentus seuiebat inimicus. ibi accipiebat limitem trucidatoris furor. illo
ducebantur a miserantibus hostibus. quibus etiam extra ipsa loca pepercerant ne
in eos incurrerent qui similem misericordiam non habebant. qui tamen etiam
ipsi alibi truces atq. hostili more seuientes. postea q̄ ad loca illa ueniebant ubi fue
rat interdictum quod alibi iure belli licuisset tota feriendi frenabatur imma
nitas et captiuandi cupiditas frangebatur. Sic euaserunt multi qui nūc xp̄ianis

53 Aesop's *Vita et Fabulae*, printed by Johann Zainer at Ulm in 1476-7

54 Zainer added fables by other authors in this edition of Aesop. This woodcut illustrates Poggio's story of the Hypocrite and the Widow

was arranged. At first Zainer was denied the right to illustrate books at all, but later he gained this privilege upon engagement to use only the services of members of the local guilds in cutting the blocks, even though it appears he was capable of doing this for himself. The Abbot Melchior, to whom we all owe so much, went a step further, and, despite all the entreaties of his friends, set up a press in the monastery with Zainer as his right-hand man. Here, in 1473, they printed the *Speculum Humanae Salvationis*, one of the most beautiful illustrated books to be created in northern Europe. In character this work is similar to the semi-block-book editions, but with a much longer text in both Latin and German, and a metrical summary by Frater Johannes who lived and worked in the same monastery. In the *Mirror of Human Salvation* all the contrasts of life are reflected, the good and the evil qualities to be found among men from Pope and Emperor to town and country labourer. The medieval love of antithesis is given full play and the two hundred woodcuts give a vigorous and charming picture of contemporary life. These cuts, so infused with all that is best in the German character, were the creations of the very spirit that produced the wood and stone carvings found in Gothic cathedrals, and the book gains immensely from the unity of character between the blocks and the type in which the text is printed. The rounded heads, the solid blacks of belts, shoes, etc., and the strong cutting marries well with the sturdy black type [figures 48, 49 & 50]. No man was better fitted to judge books of this kind and no man loved them more or with greater warmth and insight than William Morris, whose admirable essay 'On the Artistic Qualities of the Woodcut Books of Ulm and Augsburg in the Fifteenth Century' is in Vol. One of *Bibliographica*, 1895.

A few years later, about 1475-6, Zainer produced a German Bible with historiated initial letters at the opening of each book. These were closely derived from the decorations in illuminated MSS, with vigorous figures of Biblical characters surrounded by well-drawn foliage [figure 57].

It has been remarked that the railway time-tables in Burgundy read like a wine catalogue; and for the bibliophile, as he drives along the autobahn through Western Germany the signposts might almost be the index to a library of incunabula: Cologne, Mainz, Bamberg, Esslingen, Nuremberg, Augsburg and Ulm. Ulm was another city to produce remarkable woodcut books, a city already noted, as mentioned above, for the production of playing cards. It is rather sad to have to record that the Ulm printers did not meet with much worldly success; perhaps they had more difficulty in distributing their books, Ulm being a less powerful commercial city than Augsburg and cursed by frequent visitations of the plague; moreover they lacked a powerful patron such as Melchior von Stamhaim. However, these troubles did not in any way prevent Johann Zainer (a kinsman of Günther's) from producing some of the best of all woodcut books, especially Boccaccio, *De Claris Mulieribus*, 1473, and Aesop, *Vita et Fabulae*, 1476-7, both works lending themselves admirably to illustration, as can be seen from those pictures reproduced here [figures 53, 54, 55, 58]. The Aesop contains fables by other authors including the delightful Poggio. Figure 54 illustrated Poggio's story of the Hypocrite and the Widow; the Widow importunes the Hypocrite, a religious mendicant, to commit the grievous sin of fornication with her. He replies, on realizing that it is impossible to dissuade her: 'I take God to witness that the deed is yours and I am free from blame. Take this accursed flesh and use it as you will, for I will not touch it today.' In the woodcut she is about to do so. Johann Zainer's books are remarkable for their borders and initials decorated with curling leafy sprays drawn with remarkable vigour and sense of design; four hundred years later they were to influence Morris when he was drawing the decorations for the Kelmscott Press.

Once the production of illustrated books was thoroughly mastered, it was natural that printers should turn their attention to the Bible, and particularly to those editions printed

55 Boccaccio's stories of famous women are transformed by the Gothic conception of the German artist in this edition of *De Claris Mulieribus*, printed by Johann Zainer at Ulm in 1473

56 *(overleaf left)* The decorated initial letter of the 'Beatus' page from a printed Psalter, Fust and Schoeffer, Mainz, 1457

57 *(overleaf right)* Woodcut initial coloured by hand, at the opening of the Book of Job, from the Bible in German printed by Gunther Zainer at Augsburg in 1475-6

Regē magnū dñm venite a

Dñicis diebꝫ post festū ephie

Adorem⁹ dñm qui fecit nos

B

Eat

non

con

via

cath,

dit,

lūtas ei⁹: et in lege eiu

nocte, Et erit tanqȝ li

secus decursus aq̄r: qđ

¶ Ein ende hatt die vorred Vnd
hebt an das bůch Job.

¶ Das erst Capitel.

In man· was in dē land hus· mit namē iob. Vnd secht der man was eynfeltig· vnd gerecht· vnnd vorcht got vñ schyed sich võ dē úbel. Vnd im waren geboren siben sún vnd drey tŏchter· vñ sein besiczung die was sibentausent schauff vñ dreytausent kemeltyer· vnd fúnffhundert

58 A border from the same edition of *De Claris Mulieribus* as figure 55. Zainer's books are remarkable for their woodcut borders and initials. Four hundred years later, they had considerable influence on William Morris when he was designing decorations for the Kelmscott Press

in the vernacular; the first Bible in the German language had been produced at Strasbourg in 1466. Lay readers, especially those fired by the already dawning Reformation, were more likely than the clergy to have an appetite for pictures, and especially pictures of Old Testament stories. It is not surprising, therefore, that the most influential of all illustrated Bibles, that printed at Cologne in 1478 by Heinrich Quentell, was produced in two editions, each of them in a different German dialect [figure 59].

Few German woodcut books are better known than the *Nuremberg Chronicle*, printed by Anton Koberger in 1493. This large folio contains woodcuts illustrating the Bible, ecclesiastical and other history, topography, maps and views of towns. There are actually 645 different blocks, but by repeating these at intervals the total is swelled to 1809 pictures. Naturally there can be no claim to individual portraiture, the same cut being used again and again to depict different bishops or saints; and while the large double-page pictures of cities bear considerable resemblance to reality and are only used once, twenty-two other blocks of cities and countries are repeated to represent sixty-nine different places. These blocks were produced by Michael Wolgemut (who was Dürer's master) and Wilhelm Pleydenwurff. They vary in merit, but some of them are of considerable quality. Nevertheless, the great variety of size ensures that there is very little balance of pages or consistency of style; somehow one feels that this is a commercial or made-up book, the first *édi-*

tion de luxe, giving rich burgher customers the greatest possible value for their money [figure 31 & 64].

The genius which Venetian artists could bring to bear on a book may be seen in the woodcuts which illustrate Ketham, *Fascicolo di Medicina*, 1493-4 [figure 65]. Surely no other textbook has ever achieved such grave dignity; artist and engraver have combined to catch the finest spirit of a noble profession. We know hardly any more about the artists who designed book illustrations than we know about the men who illuminated manuscripts, but such important authorities as A.M. Hind and Friedrich Lippmann seriously

59 Many sophisticated people retain images of Bible stories they saw in Sunday School pictures. Almost all followed the tradition of illustration established in this German Bible, printed by H. Quentell in Cologne *c.* 1478

60 *(overleaf left)* At first this appears to be a page from an illuminated manuscript; but it is a printed text, one of a few copies on the finest vellum, illuminated by hand for a Renaissance prince

61 *(overleaf right)* Pugin and Rowlandson give a lively impression of the interest aroused by a fire in the early nineteenth century; plate from Ackermann's *Microcosm of London*

LIBRO PRIMO DELLA HISTORIA DELLE COSE FACTE DALLO INVICTISSIMO DVCA FRANCESCO SFORZA SCRIPTA IN LATINO DA GIOVANNI SIMONETTA ET TRADOCTA IN LINGVA FIORENTINA DA CHRISTOPHORO LANDINO FIORENTINO.

NE TEMPI CHE LA REGINA GIOVANNA SEconda figliuola di Carlo Re regnaua: perche era succeduta nel regno Neapolitano a Latislao Re suo fratello: elquale parti di uita sanza figliuoli: Alphonso Re daragona con grande armata mouendo di Catalogna uenne in Sicilia: Isola di suo Imperio. La cui uenuta excito gli huomini del Neapolitano regno a uarii fauori: & a diuersi consigli: & non con piccoli mouimenti di quel regno: Impero che Giouãna Regina per molti & uarii suoi impudichi amori era caduta in sõma infamia. Et desperandosi che lei femina potessi adempiere lofficio del Re: & administrare tanto regno: fece a se marito Iacopo di Nerbona Conte di Marcia: elquale per nobilita di sangue: & belleza di corpo: ne meno per uirtu era tra Principi di Francia excellente. Ma accorgendosi in breue che quello desideraua piu essere Re: che marito: & quella non molto stimaua: mosso da feminile leuita lo rifiuto: & priuo dogni administratiõe. Questo fu cagione chel suo regno: elquale per sua natura e prono alle dissensioni & discordie: arrogendouisi e nõ honesti costumi della Regina: ritorno nelle antiche factioni & partialita: & comincio ogni giorno piu a fluctuare & uacillare. Erano alcuni a quali nõ dispiaceua la signoria della dõna: perche benche il nome fussi in lei: loro nientedimeno comãdauono. Altri desiderauano: che Lodouico tertio Duca dangio: figliuolo di Lodouico elquale era nomato Re di Puglia: & di uiolante: nata della Reale stirpe daragonia: fussi adoptato dalla Regina. Costui poco auãti pe conforti di Martino tertio sõmo Pontefice: & di Sforza Attendolo excellentissimo Duca in militare disciplina: & padre di Francesco sforza de cui egregii facti habbiamo a scriuere era uenuto a liti di Campagna: Et cõgiuntosi Sforza: hauea mosso guerra alla Regina. Ma quegli che repugnauano a Lodouicho: metteuano ogni industria: che Alphonso fussi adoptato in figliuolo della Reina: accio che in Napoli fussi tal Re: che con le sue forze & di mare & di terra potessi resistere alla possa de Franciosi. Adunque in cosi uehemẽte contentione de baroni: & piu huomini del regno: Alphonso chiamato dalla Reina in herede & compagno del regno: diuẽne nõ solo illustre: ma anchora horribile: Et el nome Catelano elquale insino a quegli tempi nõ era molto noto & celebre se non a popoli marittimi: ma inuiso & odioso: comincio a crescere: & farsi chiaro. Ma & da Lodouico & da Sforza tanto ogni giorno piu erono oppressi: el Re & la Regina: che diffidãdosi nelle proprie forze: conduxono Braccio Perugino: el quale era el secondo Capitano di militia in Italia in quegli tẽpi cõ molte honoreuoli cõditioni: & maxime

Pugin & Rowlandson, del. et sculp.

J. Bluck Aquat.

FIRE IN LONDON.

XVI.&.XVII. Del la iuri

Capitulo.xvi.
Veſte coſe pcio ho decte o mia madona euſtochio accio che tu cōſideri aquā to periculo tu ſei expoſta & cū quāta prudētia nela uia didio ti biſogna anda re:acioche laſciati gli ſetieri dela iuſtitia tu nō ſia p̄ſa da gli inimici de quali tutte leco ſe ſono piene.&conducta nella terra altrui coinquinata cō morti miſerabilmēte ſia di putata cō coloro che ſono nelo iferno.ma uoglio che tu ipari doue ſia la ſapiētia do ue ſia la uirtu doue ſia la prudentia doue ſia lalongeza de la uita & el uiuere doue ſia el lume de gli ochii & la pace.accioche tu in

64 Noah directs the building of the Ark, a woodcut from the *Nuremberg Chronicle*, 1493

considered that the Ketham woodcuts may have been designed by Mantegna or Gentile Bellini.

Two books printed at Ferrara are notable for their illustrations. The *Epistles of St Jerome*, printed by Laurentius de Rubeis, 1497, opens with a fine woodcut border and a picture of the saint seated in a Renaissance study. But the main attraction of the book lies in the series of small woodcuts depicting incidents in the life of the saint. The artist must have been a man with a considerable sense of humour which he expresses through St Jerome's lion, who often sits unnoticed in a corner looking on with an expression that leaves little doubt of his feelings: he is bored, sceptical, warmly approving or angry as the occasion demands. Later in the book cuts depicting the lives of nuns give a vivid insight into fifteenth-century conventual life. In one illustration three sisters, stripped to the waist and kneeling by the altar, passively await the cat-o-nine tails about to be wielded by their superior.

The other Ferrara book, *De Claris Mulieribus* by Jacobus Philippus Foresti (Bergomensis), a history of famous women throughout the ages, is illustrated with a series of portraits. The woodcuts which portray women from ancient times have no more claim to accuracy, of course, than those in the *Nuremberg Chronicle*; but several women contemporary with the book are actually depicted from life. This precedent is all the more interesting because the ladies in question come from the little courts which formed so fascinating a feature of Renaissance life [figure 74]. Another attractive portrait from North Italy is that of Paolo Attavanti in his *Breviarium Totius Juris Canonici*, Milan 1479; this is the earliest Milanese book with a woodcut [figure 73].

The most important Florentine woodcut book is the *Epistole e Evangelii*, printed by Morgiani in 1495. Only two copies have survived, and one of those has been damaged by fire. However, while the damaged copy was in the possession of C.W. Dyson Perrins he reproduced it in facsimile for the Roxburghe Club. It opens with a splendid frontispiece followed by numerous smaller cuts of great charm [figures 71 and 75]. But Florence was not one of the greatest printing centres; indeed some important Florentine scholars had their work produced in Venice, and many of the Florentine books were tracts, romances, small volumes of poetry, works of an ephemeral nature, not collected by connoisseurs or preserved in great libraries, but read to pieces and thrown away; consequently they are now very scarce. Prominent among these is the spate of tracts by Savonarola issued during the time when Florence was dominated by this formidable monk; they are often illustrated by woodcuts of striking beauty, which are immediately recognizable as being of the Florentine 'outline style' [figure 72].

Aldus did not normally illustrate his books, but in 1499 he produced a work which may well claim to be among the most beautiful printed books of all time, a black tulip in the

65 This woodcut from a Latin version of Ketham's *Fascicolo di Medicina*, Venice 1495, is a work of art of such a high order that it is hard to believe that it simply illustrates a medical textbook

62, 63 *(opposite left)* Two woodcuts from St Jerome's Epistles, printed by Laurentius de Rubeis at Ferrara in 1497. The mood of each incident in the saint's life is reflected in the expression of the endearing lion who was his constant companion *(below)*. In the later section, a series of woodcuts demonstrate fifteenth-century conventual life *(above)*. The opening page of the book is reproduced as Figure 3

LAMBETH CAVALRY

London Pub Nov: 1. 1798. at Ackermann's Gallery. 101 Strand.

midst of his classical texts: the *Hypnerotomachia Poliphili* by Francesco Colonna. In post-Renaissance times the text of this extraordinary book has generally been regarded as a jumble of mystical nonsense which owed its reputation solely to the woodcut illustrations, just as some really bad poems have achieved immortality because Schubert set them to music. But in the last few years there has been a revision of this view. George Painter (probably the only man capable of being at once a leading authority on fifteenth-century printing and the definitive biographer of Proust) has analyzed the text in a brilliant and perceptive essay. The *Hypnerotomachia*, which means 'The Strife of Love in a Dream', is an allegory of remarkable subtlety in which Poliphilo's pursuit of his lost love in a dream symbolizes man's striving after unattainable spiritual ideals.

On the other hand E.H. Gombrich drew attention to the influence of this book on Renaissance thought and architectural theory. Among Francesco Colonna's more distinguished readers was the architect Bramante, who was deeply impressed by the theory that obelisks should be erected in front of temples to remind those going in to pray of man's mortality. By a coincidence there was already an obelisk, erected by Julius Caesar, standing to one side of the old basilica of St Peter's; and when designing the new building Bramante suggested to his patron, Julius II, that the whole cathedral should be swung round through forty-five degrees so that not only might intending worshippers be reminded of their mortality, but the obelisk erected by one Julius would serve to glorify another. Julius II was never the man to spurn immortal fame and he appreciated the intended compliment, but the proposal involved a far greater figure: St Peter himself was buried under the basilica, and the Pope refused to disturb the sacred bones. Rather more than a century later a more reasonable solution was reached when the obelisk itself was moved into the great piazza, a feat regarded as one of the outstanding achievements of Baroque engineering.

66 Rowlandson's *Loyal Volunteers* shows the gorgeous plumage in which amateur soldiers arrayed themselves while training to preserve their country and their homes from the horrors of the French Revolution

POLIPHILO QVIVI NARRA, CHE GLI PARVE ANCORA DI DORMIRE, ET ALTRONDE IN SOMNO RITROVARSE IN VNA CONVALLE, LAQVALE NEL FINE ERA SERATA DE VNA MIRABILE CLAVSVRA CVM VNA PORTENTOSA PYRAMIDE, DE ADMIRATIONE DIGNA, ET VNO EXCELSO OBELISCO DE SOPRA. LAQVALE CVM DILIGENTIA ET PIACERE SVBTILMENTE LA CONSIDEROE.

LA SPAVENTEVOLE SILVA, ET CONSTIpato Nemore euaſo, & gli primi altri lochi per el dolce ſomno che ſe hauea per le feſſe & proſternate mēbre diffuſo relicti, me ritrouai di nouo in uno piu delectabile ſito aſſai piu che el præcedente. El quale non era de monti horridi, & crepidinoſe rupe intorniato, ne falcato di ſtrumoſi iugi. Ma compoſitamente de grate montagniole di nontropo altecia. Siluoſe di giouani quercioli, di roburi, fraxini & Carpini, & di frondoſi Eſculi, & Ilice, & di teneri Coryli, & di Alni, & di Tilie, & di Opio, & de infructuoſi Oleaſtri, diſpoſiti ſecondo la ſpecto de gli arboriferi Colli. Et giu al piano erano grate ſiluule di altri ſiluatici

67 The *Hypnerotomachia* ('The Strife of Love in a Dream') by Francesco Colonna, was published in Venice by Aldus in 1499. It opens with its hero, Poliphilus, wearied by a journey through a dark and unfrequented wood, sleeping in the shade of an olive

70 *(opposite below)* The extraordinary beauty of these woodcuts, thought by so many connoisseurs to be the loveliest ever conceived, is epitomized in this example in which, with economy and simplicity, the lovers Poliphilus and Polia are re-united in an embrace of moving tenderness

But to return to the illustrations [figures 67 to 70]. All the great movements which have shaped the mind of mankind pass through an early and lyrical springtime — when it seems that every human problem can be solved by the application of the new ideals. Later, when the eternal difficulties of reality come to be faced, disillusion all too often sets in; but the *Hypnerotomachia* woodcuts express, as perfectly as any work of art, the unclouded morning, with the dew still on the grass, of the early Renaissance.

As George Painter has truly remarked:

> Gutenberg's *Forty-two-Line Bible* of 1455 and the *Hypnerotomachia* of 1499 confront one another from opposide ends of the incunable period with equal and contrasting pre-eminence. The *Gutenberg Bible* is sombrely and sternly German, Gothic, Christian and mediaeval; the *Hypnerotomachia* is radiantly and graciously Italian, classic, pagan and renascent. These are the two supreme masterpieces of the art of printing, and stand at the two poles of human endeavour and desire!

Finally, let us look at a book which combines printing on vellum and gorgeous illumination [figure 60], Simonetta's *Sforziada*, printed at Milan by Antonio Zarotto in 1490. This beautiful book brings vividly to life the brilliant, art-loving though Machiavellian world of the Italian Renaissance despots, and contains portraits of two of them. Francesco Sforza, the founder of the family, began life as a *condottiere*. While in charge of the Venetian armies he was induced to change sides in the middle of a war by the offer in marriage of Bianca, illegitimate daughter of Filippo Maria Visconti, Duke of Milan – she was eight years old at the time. In due course Francesco Sforza secured the Dukedom of Milan for himself, and among the often unscrupulous and vicious rulers of the Renaissance (the Visconti had, only too rightly, chosen the viper as their emblem) this robust, rough-mannered, able soldier of fortune stands out as a ruler of unusual integrity; Milan prospered and lived happily under his rule. As the founder of the dynasty and the hero of this book his portrait has been painted by the illuminator

68, 69 The Festival of Bacchus is celebrated with a procession, in which a symbolic green and flourishing vine, planted in a classical urn, is drawn by six panthers, accompanied by Bacchantes and followed by Old Silenus, who rides unsteadily mounted on an ass

at the beginning of the text. The portrait on the right is that of his younger son, the brilliant and sinister Ludovico, nicknamed 'Il Moro', for whom this book was illuminated; his emblem, the Moor, appears in the top margin, his arms, with the fleurs-de-lys of France on an escutcheon of pretence, at the foot of the page.

There are certain qualities of the Greek tragedy about Ludovico: few men can have been blessed with more splendid worldly opportunities. The gods, it must have seemed, were lavishing their gifts upon him. But all the time he was, unconsciously, promoting his own catastrophic downfall; for his tortuous and unscrupulous political policies brought nemesis in their train at last. The French invaded Italy and sacked Milan. The cold and imperturbable Leonardo, it is said, sat unmoved, sketching the spirals of smoke which rose from the burning city, while Ludovico was dragged off to France as a captive. He spent his last nine years at Loches, the latter part of them in a dark and subterranean dungeon cut out of the solid rock. Louis XII carried home an unparalleled treasure of artistic loot, including, there is little doubt, this book.

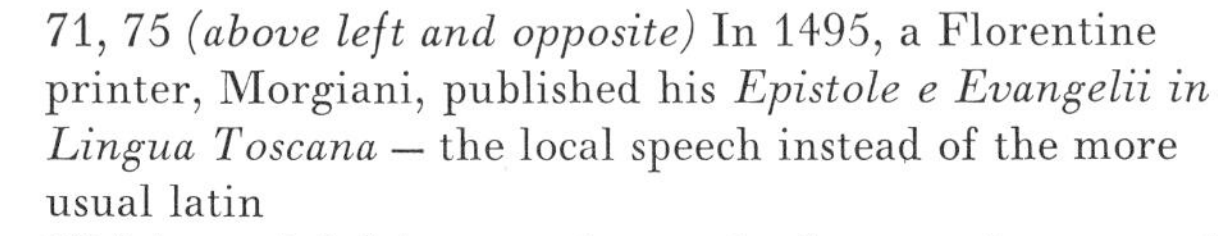

71, 75 *(above left and opposite)* In 1495, a Florentine printer, Morgiani, published his *Epistole e Evangelii in Lingua Toscana* — the local speech instead of the more usual latin

72 *(above right)* A spate of tracts by Savonarola appeared in Florence. This illustration of the reformer in his cell comes from *De Simplicitate Christianae Vitae*, 1496

73 *(below left)* The first Milanese book to contain woodcuts, the *Breviarum Totius Juris Canonici*, 1479, printed by Paolo Attavanti

74 *(below right) De Claris Mulieribus* by J. P. Foresti (Bergomensis), 1497, used portraits of contemporary women drawn from life; this one shows the Ducissa Bianchamaria Mediolani

¶ Epiſtole ⁊ Euangelii ⁊ Lectioni vulgari in lingua toſchana

F. Nash del. F. Lewis sculp.

MAGDALEN TOWER,

London Pub. Aug. 1 1814 at 101 Strand, for R. Ackermann's History of Oxford.

CHAPTER THREE

English Books with Coloured Plates 1790-1837

ENGLISH BOOKS illustrated with coloured aquatint plates are the products of one of those fortunate moments in history when, contrary to Robert Browning, the time and the place and the loved one all came together. Watercolour painting, one of England's few major contributions to the visual arts, reached the height of its creative period at the very time when the technique of aquatint printing was perfected.

It is not surprising that England, bathed in an aqueous atmosphere, should have provided the setting where watercolour painting was created; and this when the Romantic Movement in literature and the newborn feeling for the 'picturesque' in painting had turned men's eyes to the beauties of landscape, an interest stimulated by the many gentlemen who devoted their leisure to antiquarian research.

In a watercolour painting the light passes through the transparent colours and is reflected back from the white paper to the eye of the beholder. And there are times, on some morning in spring, when the sun after early rain has brought an atmosphere of brilliant clarity; so that standing before a cathedral, the contrast of the yellow stonework against the blue of a translucent sky and the green of immaculately kept grass must remind the artist, irresistibly, of a watercolour, and the book collector of an aquatint.

The England depicted in these engravings probably looked more beautiful than it has ever done before or since.

77 Fast life in the reign of George IV is the subject of C. M. Westmacott's '*The English Spy*', 1825-6. In the early chapters we see the hero at Eton, and then, as in this plate, at Oxford

76 *(opposite)* One lonely horse-drawn carriage rattles briskly over Magdalen Bridge, Oxford, in 1814, where today stationary vehicles, embedded in a traffic jam, poison the air with their fumes. Plate from Ackermann's *History of Oxford*, 1814

Much of the countryside had been transformed under the influence of Capability Brown, Repton and similar landscape gardeners. In the cities most of the buildings we admire had already been built, including many which have since been destroyed, while the general aspect had not yet succumbed to that urban sprawl which was an inevitable consequence of the Industrial Revolution. During the years preceding 1815 the Napoleonic wars provided exciting scenes of battle on both land and sea, with picturesque uniforms, and a never-ending inspiration for caricature. After Waterloo, pride in a new-found national pre-eminence, expanding success in overseas trade and freedom of movement sent many expeditions to remote and exotic countries such as China, while the colourful life and landscape of colonies such as India provided endless subjects for the artists who often accompanied important travellers and diplomatic missions.

In the late eighteenth century there were very few art schools and a number of famous painters, including Turner, Girtin and Cotman, began their careers as engravers or earned their living as aquatint colourists. This experience gave them a natural sympathy for prints and an understanding of the engraver's problems when their turn came for creating original paintings. It also gave them training in technique. Cotman's marvellous capacity for putting on watercolour washes may well have been due to his experience in working as a colourist for Ackermann, just as Rouault was influenced by his early training as a worker in stained glass and Renoir by the painting of ceramics.

While it is obvious that every single aquatint print was not coloured by an artist of genius, none the less the standard achieved was surprisingly high. In a period where there is an upsurge of creative ability, many lesser men and women are lifted by the general swell. Just as in the reign of Elizabeth I almost any statesman or even adventurer seems to have been capable of writing a well-turned sonnet, so in the early nineteenth century many people whose talents did not

quite enable them to stand on their own as original artists supported themselves as aquatint colourists and turned out very satisfactory work. And Repton tells us in *Observations on Landscape Gardening* (1803): 'The art of colouring plates in imitation of drawings has so far improved of late that I have pleasure in recording obligations to Mr Clarke, under whose direction a number of children have been employed to enrich this volume.'

Rudolf Ackermann, 1764-1834, was one of those exceptional men, who, like Diaghilev, had the perception, sympathy and capacity for organization that enabled other men of widely diverse talents and genius to combine their creative gifts in mutual achievement and provided the setting in which they could work. He seized upon the new opportunities of his time; selected artists, engravers, colourists and authors; co-ordinated their activities, and then organized a

78 Ackermann's shop, the Repository of Arts, opened in London in 1795 roughly where the Savoy Hotel now stands. It became a fashionable rendez-vous where the art-loving *beau monde* selected aquatints, books, screens, fans and other novelties.

79 It is surprising to find that the pillory was still in use at Charing Cross in the Strand as late as 1808-10, when it is shown in this plate from Ackermann's *Microcosm of London*

vast market for the distribution and sale of their work. Although he died three years before Queen Victoria came to the throne, there is something almost Victorian about Ackermann's tireless energy, industry, flair, capacity and endless devotion to his business; but for him, many of the finest aquatint books would never have been produced.

The odd thing is that Ackermann's entry into the field of publishing was so casual that it almost seems like an accident. He was born at Stolberg, Saxony, the son of a coachbuilder. As a young man he entered the family business, but worked as a designer rather than a craftsman, in

which capacity he moved first to Paris and then to London, where, in 1790, he designed the state coach, built at a cost of £7,000, for the Lord Mayor of Dublin. Later in life he produced drawings for the fantastic and elaborate car which formed the centre-piece of Nelson's funeral.

Having married an Englishwoman and founded a family, Ackermann realized that should he die young his capacity as a designer would die with him, leaving his dependants in want. To provide a more lasting means of support, in 1795 he opened a print shop in the Strand, 'The Repository of Arts', and this venture flourished beyond all expectation.

80 Many famous characters, including authors, were among the debtors who lived comfortably in the King's Bench Prison; another plate from Ackermann's *Microcosm of London*

81 The Radcliffe Library, built by James Gibbs, is here shown in Ackermann's *History of Oxford*, 1814

The first volume of Ackermann's successful magazine, also called *The Repository of Arts*, contains a print illustrating the showroom [figure 78], and the accompanying text gives us some insight into the methods of production. Many elegant but otherwise untrained French aristocrats, refugees from the Revolution, were taken on: 'Mr A. was among the first to strike out a liberal and easy method of employing them, and he had seldom less than fifty nobles, priests and ladies of distinction at work upon screens, card-racks, flower-stands, and other ornamental fancy-work of a similar nature.' When the decree allowing the return of the exiles to France was announced they hurried home, (and who can blame them?). But after 1815 a new set of refugees arrived from Spain and the good work went on.

But it would be unjust to leave a picture of Ackermann as a mere employer of sweated labour; he was a man of generous spirit, who was tireless in relieving the suffering which the ambition of Napoleon scattered over the length and breadth of Europe. After the battle of Leipzig, Ackermann raised £200,000 to help the mutilated, the homeless and the bereaved.

Ackermann's *Microcosm of London* (1808-10) three volumes quarto, with 104 coloured plates, is a book of major importance. The architectural drawings were made by Augustus Charles Pugin, a French refugee who came to London about 1798, 'driven from his country either by the horrors of the Revolution or by private reasons connected with a duel'. At that time noblemen, inspired by the Romantic movement, were demanding that their great houses should be rebuilt in the 'Gothick' manner, a style of which most architects had but a superficial knowledge, and John Nash employed Pugin, not only in his drawing office, but to travel around making drawings of Gothic buildings and details. Later in life he set up on his own, but although he trained many architects of the succeeding generation, including his famous son, Pugin's own architectural practice

was minuscule, his lasting fame resting on his consummate ability as an architectural draughtsman. By a stroke of genius Ackermann engaged Thomas Rowlandson to add human figures to the drawings which Pugin made for *The Microcosm*, so that the stately, accurate and dignified qualities of that artist are enlivened by the vitality and charm of Regency life as depicted by one of the most vigorous draughtsmen of all time. To turn the leaves of *The Microcosm* is to take a walk through London at a singularly fortunate moment, observing, as we never can in real life, the scenes of many celebrated incidents in English literature and history: the India House of Charles Lamb, the King's Bench Prison of Dickens, the Foundling Hospital of Captain Coram and Hogarth, the Guildhall bombed by the Luftwaffe, the Newgate of Harrison Ainsworth, the Carlton House of the Prince Regent, and so forth [figures 61, 79, 80].

82 Ackermann's *History of the Colleges*, 1816, portrays what are more generally known today as the 'Public Schools', as in this view of Eton

83 The statue of King Charles I at the top of Whitehall is the only feature of this plate from Papworth's *Select Views of London* in existence today. The buildings on the left were demolished to create Trafalgar Square, old Northumberland House to make way for Northumberland Avenue

Another of Ackermann's books, which may well be coupled with *The Microcosm*, is John Buonarotti Papworth's *Select Views of London* (1816) with seventy-six coloured plates. Many of the fine and lovely buildings depicted in these two books are still with us – Somerset House, St Paul's St Martin-in-the-Fields. But basically they show us a London that has passed away. Not only are there engravings of buildings now forever gone – the Pantheon, for example, or Carlton House or the Old Bailey, but even the settings of those that remain are now so changed as to be almost unrecognizable – the long unspoiled streets of Georgian houses, Berkeley Square and Lansdowne House before their pitiful mutilation, Charing Cross with old Northumberland House.... and Oxford Street. Who would ever believe Oxford Street to have been beautiful? But it was, and in some ways these books are almost too heartbreaking to look through. For here, perhaps more clearly than anywhere else, we can see for ourselves how vitally and irretrievably a hundred and fifty years of our brave new world have changed the London that Johnson and Wordsworth loved.

Three of Ackermann's most important publications, each in elephant (large) quarto, are devoted respectively to *The Colleges* (public schools) (1816) with forty-eight coloured plates; *The University of Cambridge* (1815) with seventy-nine coloured plates; and *The University of Oxford* (1814) with eighty-two coloured plates. The original watercolour drawings, some of which are in the Victoria and Albert Museum, are the work of Augustus Pugin, Frederick Mackenzie, Frederick Nash and William Westall. They were engraved by the leading aquatinters of the day. A thousand copies of each book were printed, but they become fewer and fewer every year owing to the barbarous habit, almost an industry, of breaking up the books and selling the prints separately to alumni who look back with sentimental attachment to their alma mater [figures 76, 81, 82].

Those who think of Oxford as 'the English Detroit' can

learn from Ackermann, with pleasurable surprise, that the city contains an ancient university. Embedded in this welter of noise, shoppers, heavy lorries and chain stores, lie many glorious buildings. These aquatints show the splendid city before the deluge; figure 76, drawn by Frederick Nash and engraved by George Lewis, proves that to walk over Magdalen Bridge was once a peaceful experience.

Thomas Rowlandson, 1756-1827, was the greatest of all English caricaturists and one of the most striking draughts-

84 In his *Select Views of London*, 1816, J. B. Papworth shows us Oxford Street. Could anything demonstrate more clearly the degredation which has since come over London's streetscapes?

Whene'er Death plays, He's sure to win:
He'll take each knowing Gamester in.

85, 86 *(above and opposite) The English Dance of Death* (1815-16) shows Rowlandson and Combe in sombre mood. Death is the dominating participant in every stage of human life and every scene of human activity – a theme as eternally absorbing to Rowlandson as to the artists of the *Nuremberg Chronicle* and to Holbein

men of any school or time. He expressed to perfection the bawdy, drinking, gambling, high-living and low-thinking life of the Regency, a life that he himself lived with Rabelaisian vigour; and his work gives us, perhaps better than that of any other artist, a view of the world as seen from the standpoint of the Prodigal Son. While Ackermann was a Victorian before his time, Rowlandson harks back to the unregenerate eighteenth-century world of Fielding and Smollett, which was then having one last great and glorious public fling under the Regency before going underground during the respectable days of Victoria.

It was a great stroke of luck for such a man as Rowlandson to enter into association with the steady and enterprising

Pub. June 1 1815, at R. Ackermann's, 101 Strand.

The fatal Pilot grasps the Helm,
And steers the Crew to Pluto's Realm.

London: Published Apr 1.1813 at R Ackermann's Repository of Arts, 101 Strand.
DOCTOR SYNTAX SKETCHING THE LAKE.

Ackermann, who acted virtually as his patron. Indeed, only the wide ramifications of 'The Repository of Arts' were capable of selling enough of Rowlandson's drawings to keep him financially afloat; and it was Ackermann who commissioned the greater part of Rowlandson's work in book form.

In 1809, fired by the early success of his *Repository*, Ackermann founded *The Poetical Magazine*, which had one feature of remarkable vitality. Rowlandson had produced a handful of drawings depicting the picaresque adventures of a comic schoolmaster-clergyman. When Ackermann saw these he instantly perceived their possibilities and engaged William Combe to write a rhyming text. This character soon became internationally famous (translated into German and French) as Dr Syntax. The story was produced in serial form; every month Rowlandson supplied one or two drawings of the unfortunate Syntax in some humorous adventure or misfortune. Combe had to keep pace in verse, weaving these incidents into a continuous narrative, not knowing while he wrote up the current drawing what the next one would portray. The model for Syntax may well have been William Gilpin, an artistic schoolmaster turned clergyman, Vicar of Boldre on the verge of the New Forest, a man of attractive character who published a number of tours, generally in search of picturesque scenery, which were illustrated by his own drawings reproduced in aquatint. At any rate, when the joint work appeared in book form in 1812 it was entitled: *The Tour of Doctor Syntax in Search of the Picturesque.* This met with such overwhelming success that the name of Syntax was attached to popular articles of commerce, and two sequels soon followed.

In 1815-6 the same team produced another work: *The English Dance of Death.* This is a theme which has fascinated many artists throughout the ages, and the serious subjects brought out deeper and more moving strains in Rowlandson's character, resulting in some of his best work.

Rowlandson's work for Ackermann was by no means limited to caricature, as can be seen in his splendid *Loyal Volunteers of London & Environs, Infantry and Cavalry, in their respective Uniforms* (1798-9). At that time Napoleon was as great a menace to England as Hitler was to be a century and a half later; the Loyal Volunteers, ('This Illuminated School of Mars', as they are called in the Dedication) were precursors of the Home Guard which sprang up during the last war, a citizen army trained to defend their own homes, though there is a striking contrast between the peacock uniforms of 1798 and the drab khaki of 1940.

William Combe, 1741-1823, the author of so many of Ackermann's publications, is another man whose work all too often reflected his own life. After being educated at Eton and Oxford he spent some time travelling in Italy and France. On his return home he ran swiftly through a considerable fortune by means of a style of living so extra-

87, 88 *(above and opposite) The Tour of Dr Syntax,* with rhyming text by William Combe, and coloured plates by Rowlandson, caused a furore in Regency society. The central character, Dr Syntax, was probably based on the Reverend Wm Gilpin

89, 90 *(overleaf)* The long struggle against Napoleon provided rich material for English artists and caricaturists. As the tide began to turn in favour of England and her allies, victories by land and sea were recorded in many aquatint plates

Painted by T. Whitcombe. Engraved by T. Sutherland

CAPTURE of LA TRIBUNE ... June 8th 1796.

Publish'd Feb. 1, 1817, at 48, Strand, for J. Jenkins's Naval Achievements.

W.Heath del.t T. Sutherland sculp.t

STORMING OF St. SEBASTIAN, Augt. 31st 1813.

91, 94 *(above and overleaf left)* For all its short life, Carlton House exemplified the contrast between the extravagant, art-loving Prince Regent, later George IV, and his father. Pyne's *Royal Residences* is a superb record of its sumptuous decoration

95 *(overleaf right)* The twisted strata which are so dramatic a feature of the Purbeck coast show clearly in William Daniell's view of Lulworth Cove, Dorset. In this cove John Keats, then on his way to Italy, last set foot on English soil

vagant that the world dubbed him 'Count Combe'. After a wandering career on the Continent in a series of humble jobs worthy of any picaresque fictional character, he returned to London in 1772 and supported himself as a hack writer for the next fifty years. The list of his writings in the *Dictionary of National Biography* (by no means complete) fills five columns; even so he spent most of his life as a debtor in the King's Bench Prison. Conditions there, however, can hardly have been too rigorous, for he was always waited upon by his own manservant. Mr Walter, the proprietor of *The Times*, for whom Combe did a great deal of work, offered to bail him out, but Combe turned down this opportunity 'as he did not acknowledge the equity of the claim for which he suffered imprisonment'.

But Ackermann was by no means the only publisher of such fine works, and it is not possible to do more than hint at the richness and variety of English colour plate books.

W.H. Pyne's *Royal Residences* (1819) 3 vols, quarto, with a hundred colour plates, depicts Windsor, St James's Palace, Kensington Palace, Hampton Court, Buckingham House and Frogmore, but is perhaps most valuable for its record of Carlton House, that splendid realization of the extravagant taste of the Regent which was so soon swept away. James Malton's *Picturesque and Descriptive View of the City of Dublin* (1794-5), twenty-eight plates, one of the loveliest of aquatint books, has been lyrically hymned by Sacheverell Sitwell in *British Architects and Craftsmen*.

A Voyage Round Great Britain (1814-25) by William Daniell and Richard Ayton, is one of the corner stones of English illustrated books. Strictly speaking this was a tour, not a voyage. William Daniell, one of a distinguished family of artists, started at Land's End and worked his way up the west coast; he continued for a number of years, drawing and sketching throughout the summer; then when the weather broke he would return home to produce finished watercolours and aquatints. By the time he completed his tour along the south coast and arrived back at Land's End, he had engraved 308 colour plates of very high quality and filled eight large quarto volumes. This book forms a wonderful panorama; Daniell was especially inspired by the wild western coast of Scotland and the Western Isles, but there are many charming pictures of ports and watering places which have since changed beyond all recognition.

The text of the first two volumes only is by Richard Ayton, who died at the early age of thirty-seven. Probably very few people read this, but it contains some vivid and outspoken impressions of the journey which the two men made together.

While at Whitehaven Ayton descended a coal mine, and gives an unforgettable and horrifying description of the appalling conditions in which the miners – men, women and children – worked for thirteen hours a day. Ayton's description of England and Wales in 1814-16 might well have been more highly regarded today had it not been eclipsed by the splendour of Daniell's plates [figures 13, 95].

Pride in the successful outcome of the Napoleonic wars brought two books published by James Jenkins: *The Martial Achievements of Great Britain and Her Allies, 1799 to 1815*, with fifty-two coloured plates after drawings by William Heath; and the even more attractive *Naval Achievements, 1793-1817*, with fifty-five plates after drawings by T. Whitecombe and others. C.M. Westmacott's *The English Spy* contains seventy-one coloured plates, mostly by Robert Cruikshank, though there are two by Rowlandson. This book gives a remarkable picture of fast life under the Regency, from the court of George IV at Carlton House and Brighton through the *demi-monde* to the lowest dens and gambling hells. The striking thing about this work is the freedom with which famous people are mentioned and portrayed.

Before saying farewell to the Regent we might look at *The Coronation of His Most Sacred Majesty King George the Fourth* by Sir George Nayler, Garter King of Arms.

92 'Buck House' (as it is still familiarly known in certain circles, though now transformed into Buckingham Palace) was still the comparatively humble house of the frugal, home-loving George III when Pyne's *Royal Residences* was published in 1819

93 Malton, a watercolour painter strongly influenced by Paul Sandby, made an exquisite record of Georgian Dublin in aquatint. The Custom House, built by James Gandon, is generally regarded as a masterpiece

The Hall of Entrance

CARLTON HOUSE

Lulworth Cove

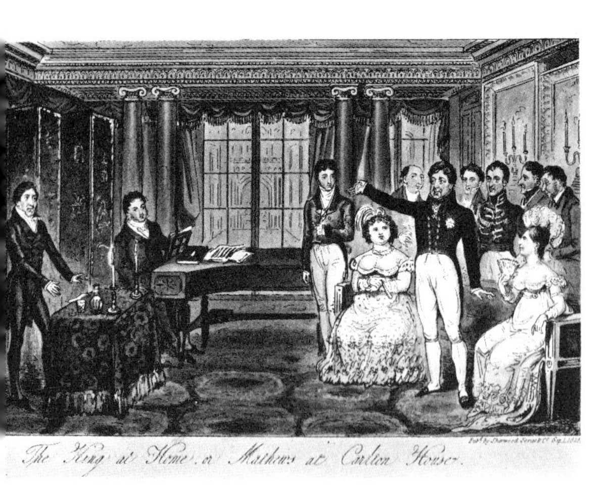

The King at Home, or Mathews at Carlton House.

96 After wallowing in the lowest of gambling hells and thieves' kitchens, Westmacott's hero is received by George IV; a plate from *The English Spy* (1825-6)

It was intended to issue this work in five parts; the first appeared in 1823, the second in 1827; but Nayler died in 1831 and the work was suspended; in 1837, H.G. Bohn acquired the plates and brought out a sumptuous work in large folio. If ever a book illustrated the boast of heraldry, the pomp of power it is this one; the forty-five plates display the leading functionaries of a coronation in full ceremonial dress.

Boydell's Thames takes its name from the publishers, John and Josiah Boydell. John Boydell, 1719-1804, was a sort of Dick Whittington character who walked from Shropshire to London in his youth and, having made a great fortune, lived to become Lord Mayor. He started by selling his own engravings at six for sixpence in the windows of toyshops, later founding a successful art gallery of his own. The original drawings for *Boydell's Thames*, which trace the river from its source to the sea in a series of seventy-six plates, were by Joseph Farington, the text by the ever-resourceful William Combe.

Humphrey Repton, 1752-1818, the celebrated landscape gardener, did much to change the landscape of the parks of gentlemen and noblemen, humanizing the rather austere style of his forerunner Capability Brown. It was Repton's custom, having surveyed an estate, to make a series of watercolour drawings, to which movable flaps were attached, showing the landscape or garden as it was and as it could be if the suggested 'improvements' were implemented. These drawings were bound up, together with a handwritten explanatory text, and handed to the landowner; they were known as 'red books' from the colour of the binding. After some years of successful practice Repton published three handsome books on landscape gardening, incorporating examples from his own 'red books' and reproducing the drawings, with hinged overslips, in coloured aquatint. Figure 99, from *Observations on the Theory and Practice of Landscape Gardening* (1803) depicts a 'View from the Fort, near Bristol', and shows Repton's plan blotting out a disagreeable

view. 'Upon the slide are shown five rods or poles, each of which are supposed to be ten feet high, and placed at different distances from the eye; these show the difference in apparent height of the same object in different situations, and of course what may be expected from trees planted of any given size at each place.'

Repton's books therefore not only record for us the English landscape, but also played a significant part in its improvement. He has the added distinction of having been mentioned by Jane Austen, in *Mansfield Park*. 'It wants improvement, ma'am, beyond anything. I never saw a place that wanted so much improvement in my life; and it is so forlorn, that I do not know what can be done with it.' [said Mr Rushworth] . . . 'Your best friend upon such an occasion,' said Miss Bertram calmly, 'would be Mr Repton, I imagine . . .' 'Smith's place is the admiration of all the country; and it was a mere nothing before Repton took it in hand. I think I shall have Repton.'

97 The magnificent masculinity of the dignitaries in the procession at the Coronation of George IV is matched with the feminine grace of the King's Herbwoman and her six maids strewing flowers

98 *(overleaf left)* This plate from *Boydell's Thames* shows Strawberry Hill, the Gothick country house created by Horace Walpole and his 'Committee of Taste'. Grander in scale and intention than a mere 'folly', it proved to be one of the most influential buildings in the revival of Gothic architecture

99 *(overleaf right)* By showing a pair of drawings, 'Before' and 'After', Repton could convince the most sceptical client of his ability to transform the ugliest prospect into a vista of picturesque beauty

J. Farington R.A. delt
STRAWBERRY HILL.
J. C. Stadler sculpt

VIEW FROM THE FORT, NEAR BRISTOL.

VIEW FROM THE FORT, NEAR BRISTOL.

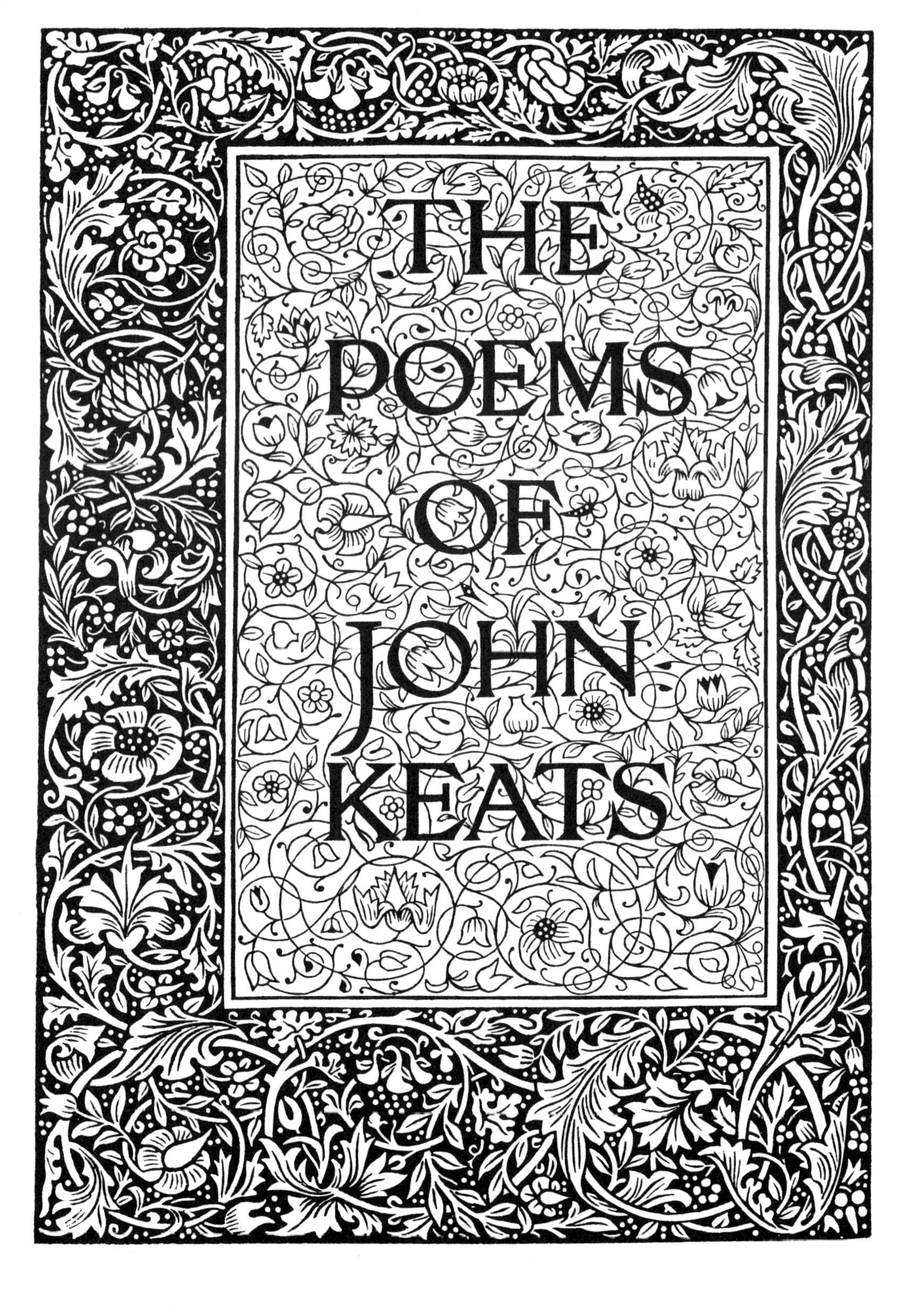
THE
POEMS
OF
JOHN
KEATS

CHAPTER FOUR

Private Presses

BY THE MIDDLE OF THE NINETEENTH CENTURY standards of design in printing had reached a very low ebb. The increasing use of machinery and the relentless competition as to who could print most cheaply contributed to this situation; but printing was not alone among the nineteenth-century arts and crafts in having reached something of a nadir. In the long run the only hope of salvation lay in rethinking the whole problem from basic principles; but working master printers had little time, and perhaps less inclination, to do this – it has been said that you can tell how little printers care about printing from the typographical standards of their own trade journals – and the revolutionary impact came from outside the trade in the form of the Private Press movement. This movement owed its inception and most of its momentum to William Morris, 1834-96.

Morris was a remarkable and lovable man of very diverse talents; a writer and poet, artist, craftsman, designer and pioneer socialist. He looked like a Norwegian sea captain, and dressed in simple clothes of blue serge which were in striking contrast to the sartorial standards of Victorian society. He was a man of great physical strength whose violent temper was easily aroused, although swiftly dispelled by the warmth of his good nature. Rossetti, a man whose reminiscences tend to be artistically rather than factually true, records that at dinner one day, just as Morris had inserted a forkful of food into his mouth, someone had the

Kelmscott
Sold by William Morris at the Kelmscott Press.

101 In order to emulate the early printers, Morris decided to sign his work with a woodcut device. Of his two principal devices, this was used for the books in larger format, such as *Beowulf*, from which this is taken

100 *(opposite)* Fine printing was revived by William Morris, who founded the Kelmscott Press in the 1890s. He designed this woodcut border, strongly influenced by the style of Erhard Ratdolt *(see figure 36)*, and used it for the title-page of this edition of Keats

THE DUKE OF WELLINGTON, as High Constable of England.

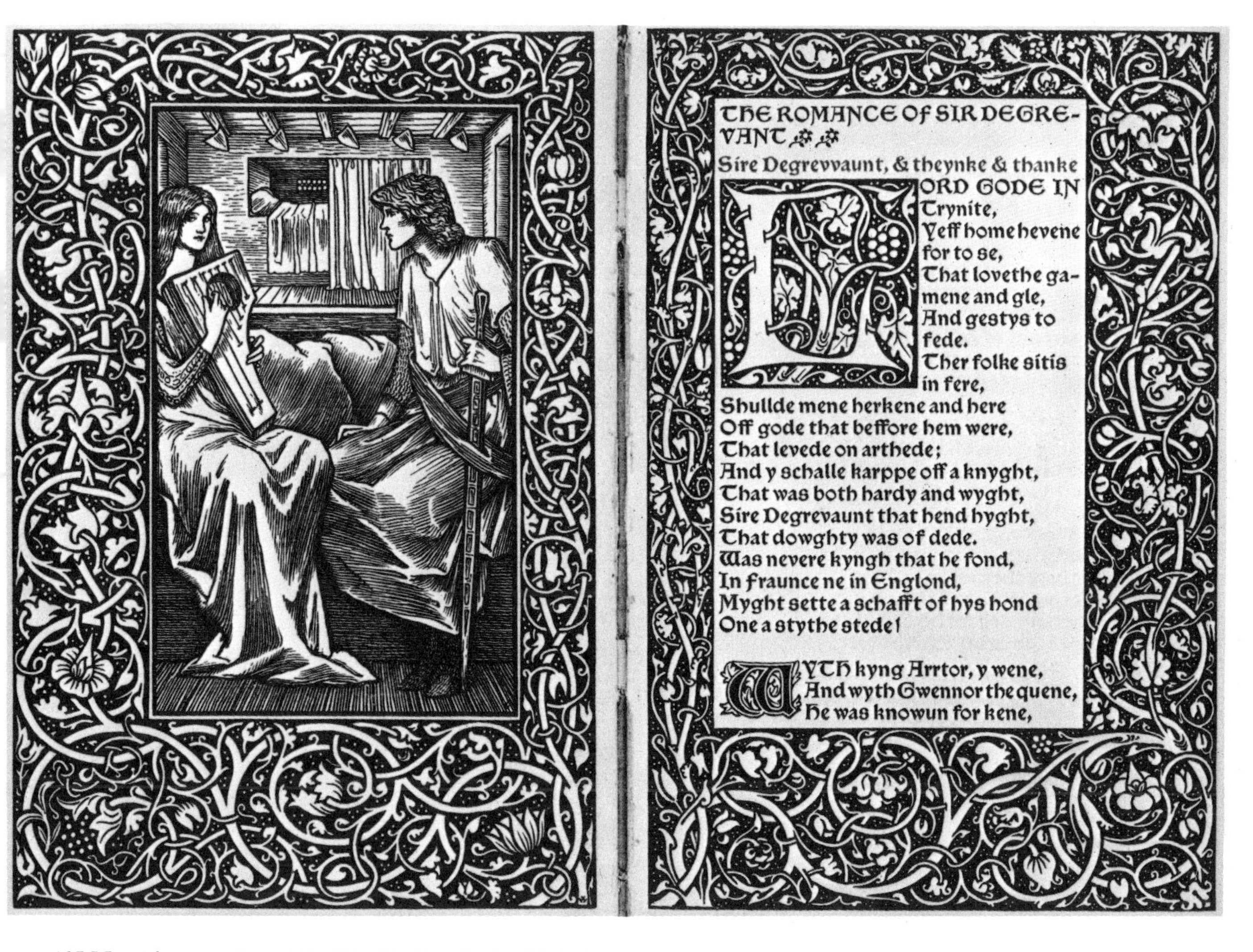

THE ROMANCE OF SIR DEGRE-
VANT
Sire Degrevvaunt, & theynke & thanke
LORD GODE IN
Trynite,
Yeff home hevene
for to se,
That lovethe ga-
mene and gle,
And gestys to
fede.
Ther folke sitis
in fere,
Shullde mene herkene and here
Off gode that beffore hem were,
That levede on arthede;
And y schalle karppe off a knyght,
That was both hardy and wyght,
Sire Degrevaunt that hend hyght,
That dowghty was of dede.
Was nevere kyngh that he fond,
In fraunce ne in Englond,
Myght sette a schafft of hys hond
One a stythe stede!

WYTH kyng Arrtor, y wene,
And wyth Gwennor the quene,
He was knowun for kene,

103 Morris's conception of the 'Double Opening', with facing pages designed as a unit. The picture is by Burne-Jones, and the text is printed in 'Troy' type

102 *(opposite)* This resplendent portrait of the Duke of Wellington in his Coronation robes, loaded with honours and Orders of Chivalry from every country in Europe, is outstanding even in the superb series of plates in Sir George Nayler's *Coronation of George IV*

temerity to criticize the work of Burne-Jones, Morris's greatest friend; in a herculean, and quite untypical effort to control his temper Morris bit on the fork, which emerged bent and twisted beyond all recognition.

On 15 November 1888, Morris attended a lecture on printing, delivered at the Arts and Crafts Exhibition by his friend Emery Walker, which finally fired him to set up his own press. It is a pleasure to pay one's tribute to Walker; he was the man whose immense practical experience, whose knowledge, taste and developed judgment were at the service of all the private presses. This immensely modest man placed his life's experience at the service of the amateur printers. Morris, with his warm-hearted generosity, wanted to name Walker as a partner; how Cobden-Sanderson, of the Doves Press, treated him, we shall see.

Morris began as usual by studying the best work of the past and based his books quite frankly on incunabula, the nearest he could get to the Middle Ages. He took as his model the roman type of Jenson and bought a copy of the famous Pliny. He had each letter of the alphabet photographed and lantern slides made so that he could study the minutest details in an enlarged form, drawing these letters over and over again until he had absorbed their spirit. Then he put the whole lot away and designed his own type. He kept these designs in a matchbox which he carried around in his pocket, taking them out at odd moments for critical examination, and showing them to perceptive friends. Walker, who was a neighbour, looked in at Morris's home every night, on his way back from work, to discuss and guide progress. While the type was being cast Morris set to work designing decorated borders and initials, printers' flowers and a colophon [figure 101]. Here again he was influenced by the early books in his own splendid library, especially the work of Erhard Ratdolt of Venice and Johann Zainer of Ulm. The first book to be started, though not the first to be completed, was the *Golden Legend* of Jacobus

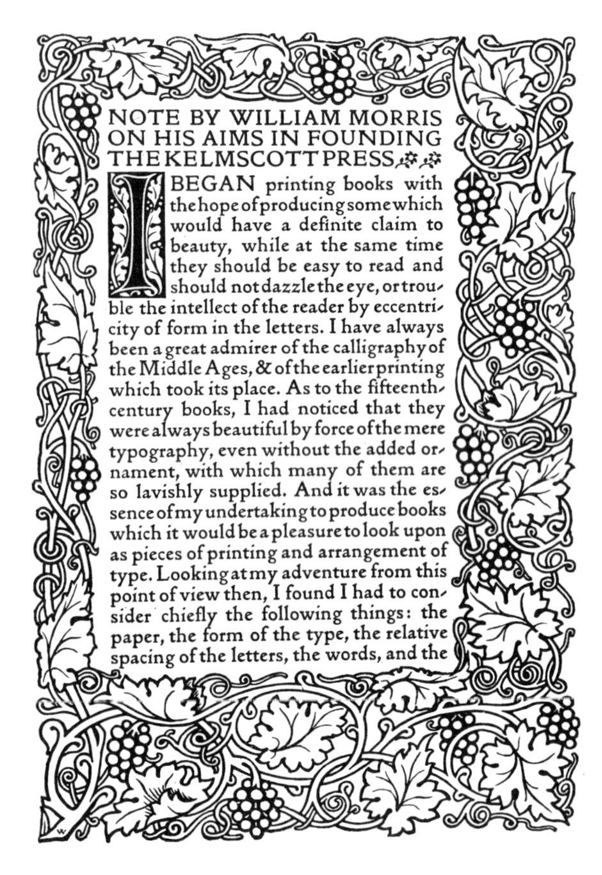
NOTE BY WILLIAM MORRIS ON HIS AIMS IN FOUNDING THE KELMSCOTT PRESS

I BEGAN printing books with the hope of producing some which would have a definite claim to beauty, while at the same time they should be easy to read and should not dazzle the eye, or trouble the intellect of the reader by eccentricity of form in the letters. I have always been a great admirer of the calligraphy of the Middle Ages, & of the earlier printing which took its place. As to the fifteenth-century books, I had noticed that they were always beautiful by force of the mere typography, even without the added ornament, with which many of them are so lavishly supplied. And it was the essence of my undertaking to produce books which it would be a pleasure to look upon as pieces of printing and arrangement of type. Looking at my adventure from this point of view then, I found I had to consider chiefly the following things: the paper, the form of the type, the relative spacing of the letters, the words, and the

104 The Kelmscott 'Golden' type was based on that of the fifteenth-century Venetian printer, Jenson. This page should be compared with figure 38

Voragine; this book gave its name to Morris's roman, which he christened the Golden type [figure 104]. But he was not content to work for ever in roman; he longed to express himself in gothic, and before long he had designed the Troy type, based, more or less, on the gothic types of Schoeffer, Zainer and Koberger.

Morris named his venture the Kelmscott Press after his lovely country house, Kelmscott Manor, near Lechlade in the Cotswolds. His original intention was to print only a few copies of each book and give them away among his friends; but when the new activity was mentioned in the public press, and when first enquiries and then orders came flowing in, it was decided to widen the scope and print a few hundred copies for sale. Morris, who didn't really give a damn for anyone, printed his own favourite books without any consideration as to whether they were likely to be in demand with the general reading public. It is true that he included Keats, Shelley, Coleridge, and, of course, Ruskin; but there is a high proportion of medieval books dear to his heart: *The Recuyell of the Historyes of Troye*, *Reynard the Foxe*, *The Order of Chivalry*, *Godefrey of Boloyne*, *Psalmi Penitentiales* and *Beowulf*.

But from the very earliest days of the Kelmscott Press Morris was working up to his masterpiece, an edition of Chaucer, his favourite author and master, a tribute which would express the devotion of a lifetime [figure 106]. Work on this book continued for five years. Morris had Chaucer in mind when he designed the Troy type, and sample pages were set up; but this fount was found to be too large for the purpose, so it was recut in a smaller size as the Chaucer type. In July 1892, the first trial page was printed, and as it was found to be satisfactory, work went ahead. The *Kelmscott Chaucer* represents the climax of the private press movement; it has been chosen again and again as the most sumptuous example of English printing. Thus, when the Library of Tokyo University was destroyed by an earthquake and English scholars met to decide on a worthy 'foundation stone' for presentation to the new library, the *Kelmscott Chaucer* was their choice. Bernard Shaw, who regarded Morris as the greatest man he had ever met ('... and I who say this have met most of the great men of my time ...'), gave a copy to Rodin, speaking of it as a worthy gift for a great artist.

105 Morris planned to follow the *Kelmscott Chaucer* with a splendid edition of his other favourite author, Froissart, but his early death put an end to this project.

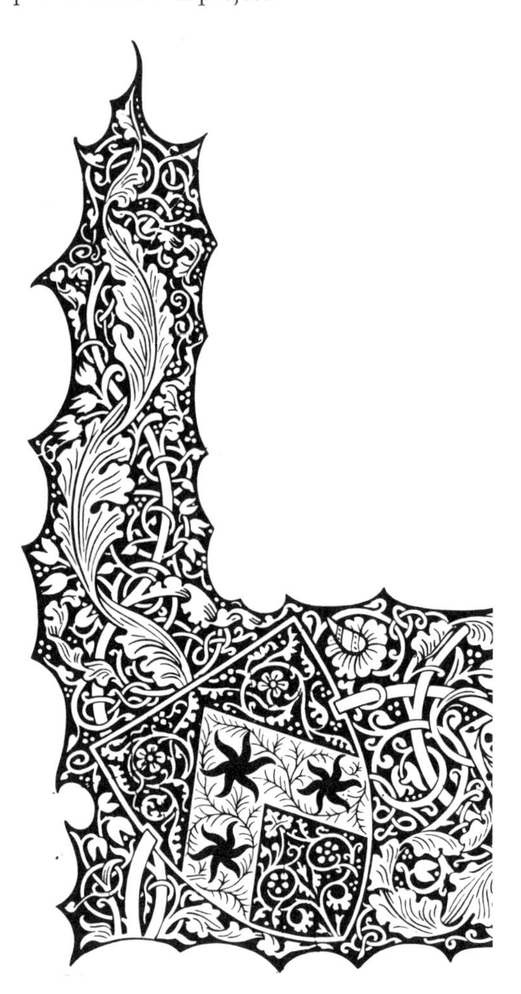

When the productions of the Kelmscott Press first appeared in the bookshops they made an immense impact; here were people accustomed to the grey pages of late Victorian printing, and along came those wonderful books with the rich blocks of black type on gleaming white handmade paper, the initials and borders rioting with decoration.

And yet, on this side idolatry, one must listen to the devil's advocate. The chief purpose of books is to be read, and to some extent Kelmscotts are beautiful *objets d'art* rather than books. Yet, as a bookseller who has been handling them for forty years, I cannot help observing what a high proportion of Kelmscott Press books have never been read, and indeed, seventy years later, many of them remain 'unopened'.

In many ways Morris was swimming against the tide: his return to gothic type when the whole movement of Europe has been towards roman; the over-exuberance of decoration which distracts the reader's eye from the text; the handmade paper which is too heavy for normal use; the insistence on small editions produced by hand. Indeed this is the contradiction of Morris's later life; his immense compassion and generous character made him want all men to share more fully in the good things of life, yet he fought against the machinery by which, alone, this end could be achieved. All these criticisms, though for a man to whom Morris is a hero this is hard to admit, contain a strong degree of truth. But none of them detract from his key position in the history of modern printing. His return to basic principles, his insistence on the finest materials used with the greatest possible care, and combined with every consideration for each other, his conception of the double opening, not the single page as the unit of design, these and many other factors have extended the influence of Morris far beyond his native shores, and especially to Germany and America.

The comparatively early death of Morris brought the Kelmscott Press to a premature end; his friends and collaborators completed the books which were actually in hand but attempted no new ones, apart from a bibliography.

106 Morris's lifelong devotion to the Middle Ages and the poetry of Chaucer found their expression in this edition, the *magnum opus* of the Kelmscott Press

the works of Geoffrey Chaucer now newly imprinted

HERE BEGINNETH THE TALES OF CANTERBURY AND FIRST THE PROLOGUE THEREOF

WHAN THAT Aprille with his shoures soote
The droghte of March hath perced to the roote,
And bathed every veyne in swich licour,
Of which vertu engendred is the flour;
Whan Zephirus eek with his swete breeth
Inspired hath in every holt and heeth
The tendre croppes, and the yonge sonne
Hath in the Ram his halfe cours yronne,
And smale foweles maken melodye,
That slepen al the nyght with open eye,
So priketh hem nature in hir corages;
Thanne longen folk to goon on pilgrimages,
And palmeres for to seken straunge strondes,
To ferne halwes, kowthe in sondry londes;
And specially, from every shires ende
Of Engelond, to Caunterbury they wende,
The hooly blisful martir for to seke,
That hem hath holpen whan that they were seeke.

BIFIL that in that seson on a day,
In Southwerk at the Tabard as I lay,
Redy to wenden on my pilgrymage
To Caunterbury with ful devout corage,
At nyght were come into that hostelrye
Wel nyne and twenty in a compaignye,
Of sondry folk, by aventure yfalle
In felaweshipe, and pilgrimes were they alle,
That toward Caunterbury wolden ryde.

IN THE BEGINNING GOD CREATED THE HEAVEN AND THE EARTH. ¶ AND THE EARTH WAS WITHOUT FORM, AND VOID; AND DARKNESS WAS UPON THE FACE OF THE DEEP, & THE SPIRIT OF GOD MOVED UPON THE FACE OF THE WATERS. ¶ And God said, Let there be light: & there was light. And God saw the light, that it was good: & God divided the light from the darkness. And God called the light Day, and the darkness he called Night. And the evening and the morning were the first day. ¶ And God said, Let there be a firmament in the midst of the waters, & let it divide the waters from the waters. And God made the firmament, and divided the waters which were under the firmament from the waters which were above the firmament: & it was so. And God called the firmament Heaven. And the evening & the morning were the second day. ¶ And God said, Let the waters under the heaven be gathered together unto one place, and let the dry land appear: and it was so. And God called the dry land Earth; and the gathering together of the waters called he Seas: and God saw that it was good. And God said, Let the earth bring forth grass, the herb yielding seed, and the fruit tree yielding fruit after his kind, whose seed is in itself, upon the earth: & it was so. And the earth brought forth grass, & herb yielding seed after his kind, & the tree yielding fruit, whose seed was in itself, after his kind: and God saw that it was good. And the evening & the morning were the third day. ¶ And God said, Let there be lights in the firmament of the heaven to divide the day from the night; and let them be for signs, and for seasons, and for days, & years: and let them be for lights in the firmament of the heaven to give light upon the earth: & it was so. And God made two great lights; the greater light to rule the day, and the lesser light to rule the night: he made the stars also. And God set them in the firmament of the heaven to give light upon the earth, and to rule over the day and over the night, & to divide the light from the darkness: and God saw that it was good. And the evening and the morning were the fourth day. ¶ And God said, Let the waters bring forth abundantly the moving creature that hath life, and fowl that may fly above the earth in the open firmament of heaven. And God created great whales, & every living creature that moveth, which the waters brought forth abundantly, after their kind, & every winged fowl after his kind: & God saw that it was good. And God blessed them, saying, Be fruitful, & multiply, and fill the waters in the seas, and let fowl multiply in the earth. And the evening & the morning were the fifth day. ¶ And God said, Let the earth bring forth the living creature after his kind, cattle, and creeping thing, and beast of the earth after his kind: and it was so. And God made the beast of the earth after his kind, and cattle after their kind, and every thing that creepeth upon the

27

105 Morris planned to follow the *Kelmscott Chaucer* with a splendid edition of his other favourite author, Froissart, but his early death put an end to this project

But the closure of the Kelmscott Press fired another man to start a press of his own. T.J. Cobden-Sanderson, 1840-1922, the founder of the Doves Press, was a man of different character from Morris. He began life as a barrister, a profession in which he showed considerable ability; but in middle life, in 1881, he decided to abandon the Bar and do creative work with his hands; a more striking decision then than it would be today. He was in close touch with the Morris circle whose ideals of craftsmanship and socialism he shared; indeed it was Cobden-Sanderson who thought up the very title 'Arts and Crafts'.

Cobden-Sanderson was sixty when he entered into partnership with Emery Walker in founding the Doves Press. Between them, though Walker took the lion's share where designing was concerned, they evolved a type of great beauty, also based on Jenson, but somewhat lighter than Morris's Golden type, a factor which enabled them to use handmade paper which was less bulky and more suitable for book work. With this type they printed books of austere but great beauty. In contrast to the lavish black ornament of the Kelmscott Press, there was no decoration, unless one counts an occasional coloured, though undecorated initial. (Once, when a client had complained at what she considered a high price for a comparatively plain binding, Cobden-Sanderson retorted 'I charge as much for my restraint as for my elaboration'.) They relied on faultless presswork, the beauty of the type and the perfect design and balance of their pages. Their masterpiece, the *Doves Bible*, 1903-5, in five folio volumes, ranks with the *Kelmscott Chaucer* as one of the twin masterpieces of the movement, and it has dated the less [figure 107]. Cobden-Sanderson's pursuit of the ideals laid down in *The Book Beautiful* had been achieved. If Morris represented the exuberant vitality of gothic, the Doves Press worked with a restraint which was classic.

It would have seemed impossible that any man could quarrel with the gentle-natured Emery Walker, but Cobden-

Sanderson achieved this seemingly unattainable feat. In 1909 the partnership was dissolved and Cobden-Sanderson continued to print alone. The question naturally arose as to who owned the Doves type; this remained in Cobden-Sanderson's possession as he was responsible for the day-to-day conduct of the press which operated on his premises. Sydney Cockerell, the friend of both men, acting as a sympathetic and skilful negotiator, found a solution; he brought both men to agree that while Cobden-Sanderson should retain the type during his lifetime, it should pass after his death to Emery Walker, who was eleven years younger.

In 1916 Cobden-Sanderson printed his *Catalogue Raisonné*, the last book to come from the Doves Press, in which appeared the following statement:

> CONSECRATIO QUAE OFFERTUR AB HOMINE NON REDIMETUR NEC VENDETUR SED MORTE MORIETUR. To the bed of the RIVER THAMES, the River on whose banks I have printed all my printed Books, I, THE DOVES PRESS, bequeath The Doves Press Fount of Type, – the punches, matrices, and the type in use at The Doves Press at the time of my death. And may the River, in its tides and flow, pass over them to and from the great sea for ever and ever, or until its tides and flow for ever cease; then may they share the fates of all the worlds and pass from change to change for ever upon the Tides of Time, untouched of other use.

This threat Cobden-Sanderson carried out, early in 1917, going night after night, 'watched only by the stars', and pitching the whole lot over Hammersmith Bridge. The first batch lodged itself on an inaccessible ledge of one of the piers; another narrowly missed a barge that was passing under the bridge – an incident which would have appealed to Morris, who loved to indulge in great swearing matches with the bargees. This extraordinary action deprived Walker of his share in the type and broke the promise given to Cockerell. Cobden-Sanderson is a curiously mixed character: on the one hand he was an idealist who gave up what

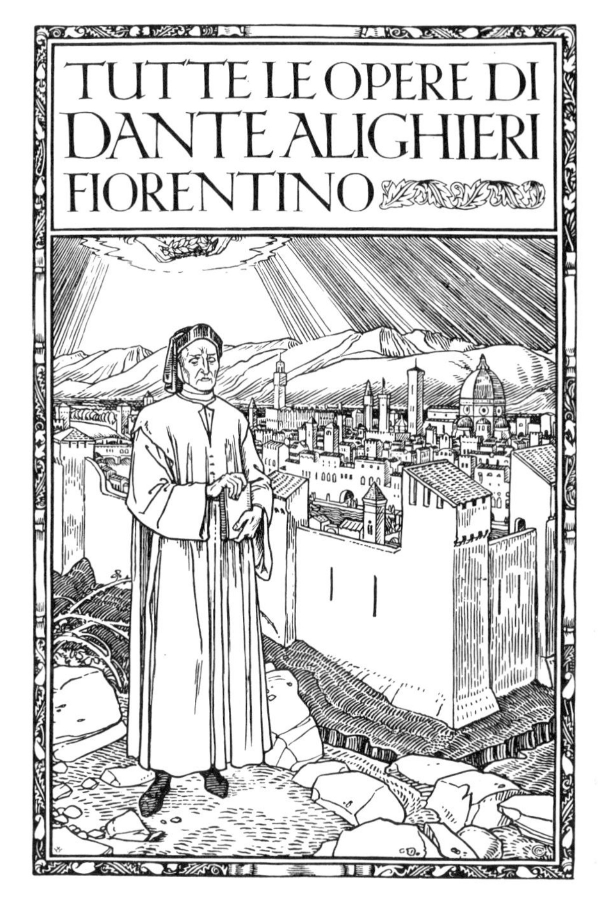

108 The *Ashendene Dante*, illustrated with woodcuts by C. M. Gere

QUI COMINCIA IL LIBRO DELLA VITA NUOVA DI DANTE. CAPITOLO PRIMO.

IN QUELLA PARTE del libro della mia memoria, dinanzi alla quale poco si potrebbe leggere, si trova una rubrica, la quale dice: Incipit Vita Nova. Sotto la quale rubrica io trovo scritte le parole, le quali è mio intendimento d'assemprare in questo libello, e se non tutte, almeno la loro sentenza. Nove fiate già, appresso al mio nascimento, era tornato lo cielo della luce quasi ad un medesimo punto, quanto alla sua propria girazione, quando alli miei occhi apparve prima la gloriosa donna della mia mente, la quale fu chiamata da molti Beatrice, i quali non sapeano che si chiamare. Ella era già in questa vita stata tanto, che nel suo tempo lo cielo stellato era mosso verso la parte d'oriente delle dodici parti l'una d'un grado: sì che quasi dal principio del suo anno nono apparve a me, ed io la vidi quasi alla fine del mio nono anno. Ella apparvemi vestita di nobilissimo colore, umile ed onesto, sanguigno, cinta ed ornata alla guisa che alla sua giovanissima etade si convenia. In quel punto dico veracemente che lo spirito della vita, lo quale dimora nella segretissima camera del cuore, cominciò a tremare sì fortemente, che apparia ne' menomi polsi orribilmente; & tremando disse queste parole: Ecce Deus fortior me, qui veniens dominabitur mihi. In quel punto lo spirito animale, il quale dimora nell' alta camera, nella quale tutti li spiriti sensitivi portano le loro percezioni, si cominciò a maravigliare molto, & parlando spezialmente allo spirito del viso, disse queste parole: Apparuit iam beatitudo vestra. In quel punto lo spirito naturale, il quale dimora in quella parte, ove si ministra lo nutrimento nostro, cominciò a piangere, & piangendo disse queste parole: Heu miser! quia frequenter impeditus ero deinceps. D'allora innanzi dico ch' Amore signoreggiò l'anima mia, la quale fu sì tosto a lui disposata, e cominciò a prendere sopra me tanta sicurtade e tanta signoria, per la virtù che gli dava la mia imaginazione, che mi convenia fare compiutamente tutti i suoi piaceri. Egli mi comandava molte volte, che io cercassi per vedere quest'angiola giovanissima: ond'io nella mia puerizia molte fiate l'andai cercando; e vedeala di sì nobili e laudabili portamenti, che certo di lei si potea dire quella parola del poeta Omero: Ella non pare figliuola d'uomo mortale, ma di Dio. Ed avvegna che la sua immagine, la quale continuamente meco stava, fosse baldanza d'amore a signoreggiarmi, tuttavia era di sì nobile virtù, che nulla volta sofferse, che Amore mi reggesse senza il fedele consiglio della ragione in quelle cose, là dove cotal consiglio fosse utile a udire. E però che soprastare

bi

I

109 A page from the *Ashendene Dante*, printed in type based on that of Sweynheym and Pannartz, shown in figure 35

might well have become a lucrative career at the bar in order to devote himself to his ideals of craftsmanship; he was a socialist at a time when very few members of the middle classes gave themselves to that cause; and yet through all this there ran a streak of ruthless selfishness and ungovernable egoism that led him to an action of which many a self-confessed money-maker would have been ashamed.

The third of the great trio of handpresses, the Ashendene, was founded by C.H. St John Hornby in 1894. It was Hornby's boyhood ambition to print fine books, and his enthusiasm was inflamed when he visited William Morris at the Kelmscott Press in 1893. At first, assisted by his family, he printed in a summer-house at Ashendene in Hertfordshire, using Caslon type; but in 1899 he moved to Shelley House on the Chelsea Embankment. (It is curious that all three presses should have been on the banks of the Thames within a few miles of each other.) Here he commissioned his own type, designed by Emery Walker and S.C. Cockerell and cut by E.P. Prince, who had cut the Kelmscott types. It was modelled on the first type of Sweynheym and Pannartz and called, therefore, Subiaco; it is a rich black calligraphic semi-roman and although rather mannered it combines well to make a fine black page. In this type Hornby printed his first really big book, a splendid folio Dante, which took three years to produce, coming out in 1909 [figure 109]. Aldus's motto, 'Hasten Slowly', might well have been Hornby's; the Kelmscott Press lasted less than a decade, the Doves less than two, yet in forty years Hornby printed fewer books than either, about forty in all, excluding minor pieces. But his books illustrate the virtues of slow work and small output; and the last productions from this press, such as the *Ecclesiasticus* of 1932, show an excellence of press work which has never been surpassed. His choice of titles, all personal favourites, are witness to the breadth of his culture: among the classics, Virgil, Horace, Apuleius and Thucydides; among the Italians, St Francis, St Clare,

Dante and Boccaccio; among English writers, Bacon, Chaucer, Malory, Milton and Spenser; and in other fields, *Omar Khayyam*, *Ecclesiasticus* and *Don Quixote*.

The Eragny Press stands a little to one side of the main stream of English private presses. Its founder, Lucien Pissarro, 1863-1944, was the son of Camille Pissarro, the Impressionist painter. Being the eldest of his family by about ten years, Lucien became almost a fellow-painter with his father and his work was shown in the last Impressionist Exhibition of 1886. His desire to produce illustrated books met with no encouragement in Paris, where his style of wood-engraving was unacceptable to the academic conventions then ruling; indeed the one commission which he did receive, in the *Revue Illustrée*, brought down such a storm of protest on the editor's head that the latter would have no more to do with him. Feeling, rightly as it turned out, that his style of work would meet with a more sympathetic reception in England, Pissarro moved to London, where he was welcomed in the circle which gathered round Charles Ricketts and Charles Shannon in their studio in The Vale, Chelsea; they published Pissarro's woodcuts in their magazine the *Dial*, and brought out the portfolio of woodcuts which he had planned for so long. Ricketts, who had already founded the Vale Press, generously allowed Pissarro to use his type, so that the first sixteen books came from the Vale Press but with the Eragny pressmark.

When Ricketts closed the Vale Press in 1904 – also throwing his equipment into the Thames, which must have become almost clogged with type – Pissarro designed a fount of his own, the Brook type, named after Stamford Brook, Hammersmith, where he lived and worked. By this time the neglect of his fellow countrymen was a thing of the past and he received considerable support from other parts of the Continent; but the declaration of war in 1914 cut him off from many of his patrons, materials were hard to come by, and the Eragny Press came to an end.

AL NOME DEL NOSTRO SIGNORE GESU CRISTO CROCIFISSO E DELLA SUA MADRE VERGINE MARIA.

IN QUESTO LIBRO SI CONTENGONO CERTI FIORETTI, MIRACOLI, ED ESEMPLI DIVOTI DEL GLORIOSO POVERELLO DI CRISTO, MESSER SANTO FRANCESCO, E DALQUANTI SUOI SANTI COMPAGNI, A LAUDE DI GESU CRISTO. AMEN.

110 In the late nineteenth and early twentieth centuries a great influence on English cultural life was the love of Italian art, fostered by much residence in Florence and other centres, and the language was widely spoken in such circles. St John Hornby subscribed to this and printed several books in Italian at his Ashendene Press, including this edition of St Francis

111 With this device, the French artist Lucien Pissarro and his wife Esther signed the books they printed in London

RIQUET À LA HOUPPE. I.

IL ÉTOIT une fois une reine qui accoucha d'un fils si laid et si mal fait, qu'on

Both Camille and Lucien Pissarro had been greatly influenced by Seurat and his ideas about the division of colour; and although Lucien's woodcuts are by no means in a *pointilliste* style the influence of the Ecole de Paris is plain to see. He was also in touch with the French Symbolist movement in poetry with its theories regarding the symbolism of colour, and he had known Oscar Wilde, who held similar views, during his early days in London. Pissarro and his wife Esther met with many technical difficulties in putting these ideas into practice; but they produced a series of little books of great charm printed in a number of delicate colours. Until the last few years these books have been curiously undervalued, but that happy opportunity for discerning book-collectors is now over and prices have risen accordingly [figures 111 & 112].

The Golden Cockerel Press, founded by Harold Taylor in 1920, has passed through the hands of several owners, each of whom has expressed his own personality and ideas, and it has given constant opportunities to a whole series of wood-engravers, Blair Hughes-Stanton, David Jones, Paul Nash, Eric Ravilious, Reynolds Stone and many others. But its most striking period occurred in the late 'twenties and early 'thirties, when there was a remarkable collaboration between Robert Gibbings, the then owner of the press, and Eric Gill. Their masterpiece was *The Four Gospels*, a book which can be placed in the same group as the *Kelmscott Chaucer* and the *Doves Bible* [figure 113]. The fact that the type and woodcuts were all the work of the same artist gives it a unity of conception rarely found. Robert Gibbings gave a delightful account of the genesis of the book in *The Book Collector*, Summer 1953:

> Before any blocks could be cut the type had to be set . . . I would spend hours with the compositors . . . Eric was the perfect collaborator . . . I would send him the proofs and on these he would build his designs, fitting his figures to the spaces determined by the type and allowing his fancy to spread into any quarter that

offered itself . . . Like many another man who is supreme at his job, Eric was essentially modest, and always ready to listen to another man's ideas . . . ready to accept a suggestion, as he was always capable of carrying it to a wonderful fruition . . . He did some splendid work for his own firm in later years, but I like to think that those engravings that he did for our edition of the Gospels were the greatest that he ever produced . . .

In 1923 two events occurred which profoundly affected English production. Stanley Morison joined the Monotype Corporation and Francis Meynell founded the Nonesuch Press. The Nonesuch was to implement an entirely new conception of private presses. Hitherto every process had been carried out by hand, so that the care and labour involved necessarily limited each edition to about three hundred copies; moreover, the scope of production was limited by the specially designed and privately owned founts of type, generally only two or three. By 1923, and more and more as Stanley Morison's influence got under way, many commercial printing houses were in possession of fine types. Meynell achieved success because he perceived and exploited the new opportunities, firstly by designing attractive books of widely differing kinds according to the individual possibilities offered by numerous printing houses; in this he used not only a variety of types but diverse ways of reproducing illustrations by Stephen Gooden, E. McKnight Kauffer, Paul Nash and other artists of striking ability. Secondly, he made full use of machine printing to issue much larger numbers – Tennyson's *In Memoriam* came in an edition of 1875 copies – thus offering Nonesuch productions at very moderate prices to a wider public than had ever bought fine books before.

In the first Nonesuch prospectus Meynell proclaimed his intention 'to choose and make books according to a triple ideal; significance of subject, beauty of format, and moderation of price'. And looking back after the first hundred books had been published he reflected, in *The Nonesuch*

beheld the linen clothes laid by themselves, and departed, wondering in himself at that which was come to pass.

BEHOLD, TWO OF THEM WENT THAT SAME DAY TO A VILLAGE CALLED EMMAUS, WHICH WAS FROM JERUSALEM ABOUT THREE-score furlongs. And they talked together of all these things which had happened. And it came to pass, that, while they communed together and reasoned, Jesus himself drew near, and went with them. But their eyes were holden that they should not know him. And he said unto them, What manner of communications are these that ye have one to another, as ye walk, and are sad? And the one of them, whose name was Cleopas, answering said unto him, Art thou only a stranger in Jerusalem, and hast not known the things which are come to pass there in these days? And he said unto them, What things? And they said unto him, Concerning Jesus of Nazareth, which was a prophet mighty in deed and word before God and all the people: And how the chief priests and our rulers delivered him to be condemned to death, & have crucified him. But we trusted that it had been he which should have redeemed Israel: and beside all this, to day is the third

208

113 Eric Gill conceived every page of the Golden Cockerel's *Four Gospels* as an entity. He engraved the opening words of each chapter on wood, filling the lettering with stylized figures in perfect harmony with the type he himself had designed and composed

112 *(opposite)* The initials in Eragny Press books were coloured in delicate pastel shades, in contrast to the bolder reds and blues of other presses

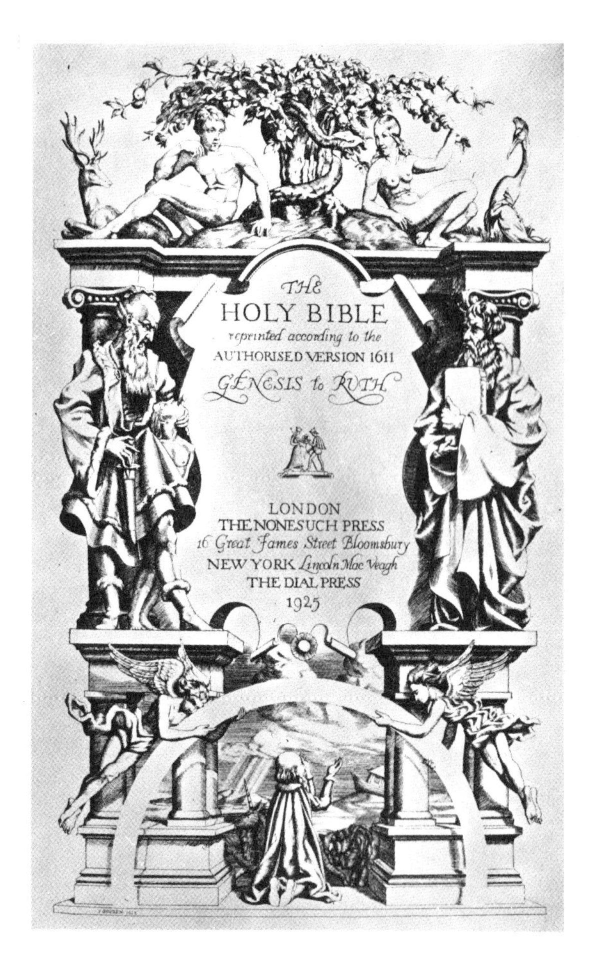

114 By the intelligent application of machine printing, the Nonesuch Press, in the period between the wars, was able to publish larger editions and bring fine books within the purse of a wider public. The title-page of this Bible is a copperplate engraving by Stephen Gooden

115 *(opposite above)* The Nonesuch Press had a lively and charming series of printers' devices. This one was designed and engraved by Stephen Gooden

116 *(opposite below)* A coloured decoration by Albert Rutherston for the *Weekend Book*, Nonesuch Press, 1928

Century: 'our stock-in-trade has been the theory that mechanical means could be controlled to serve fine ends; that the machine in printing was a controllable tool; to be designers, specifiers, rather than manufacturers; architects of books rather than builders.'

A major factor in the Nonesuch achievement was the intelligence with which the widely varying texts were chosen. Far too many private presses content themselves with producing yet further de luxe editions of *Omar Khayyam* and *Daphnis and Chloe*. The directors of the Nonesuch Press were in tune with the literary tastes of the more perceptive and sensitive spirits of their own time: with the reviving interest, for example, in the seventeenth century. In this field they produced works by Donne, Hervey, Bunyan, Burton, Evelyn, Henry King, Marvell, Milton, Izaak Walton and the dramatists Congreve, Wycherley, Vanbrugh and Dryden, edited by such scholars as Geoffrey Keynes, John Hayward, John Sparrow, Montague Summers and others. In some cases there was no really well-edited edition before the Nonesuch; in almost all cases their editions, such as Geoffrey Keynes's *Blake* and A.W. Lawrence's *Herodotus*, became the best [figures 114-16, 118].

Outside England, the private press movement has had most influence in Germany and America. Indeed, in Bruce Rogers America produced one of the most outstanding of modern typographers. His greatest importance lies, perhaps, in his having managed, as Paul Beaujon puts it, 'to steal the Divine Fire which glowed in the Kelmscott Press books, and somehow to be the first to bring it down to earth'. Bruce Rogers, like Morris, designed his own ornament as well as his type, and in one respect he went even further, designing the bindings in which his books were clothed. From 1903 to 1912 he directed the Riverside Press, Cambridge, Mass., where he produced a monumental three-volume edition of Montaigne, which gave its name to his Montaigne type. This type, like so many others, was based on Jenson's, the actual model being the latter's Eusebius. Bruce Rogers later designed an even finer type, the Centaur. His influence extended far beyond his own country, not only through the example of his own productions, widely though these were admired. For many years he acted as adviser to the Cambridge University Press (England); and it was under his direction that the Oxford University Press produced one of the outstanding examples of twentieth-century printing, their *Lectern Bible*, a masterpiece of apparent simplicity set in his own Centaur type.

Daniel Berkeley Updike was a man in the true scholar-printer tradition. Though he was not himself a designer of type, under his direction the Merrymount Press, Boston, achieved the very highest standards. Perhaps his work has received less attention from connoisseurs than its merits deserve, and possibly this neglect is because his books were not *éditions de luxe*, printed on expensive handmade paper in severely restricted numbers. Instead, as Mr Winship has said, '...his outstanding achievement was the uninterrupted production of printed matter that met the desires as well as the requirements of ordinary readers more completely as well as more satisfactorily than anyone else had done.' But Updike's name is honoured wherever printing is seriously studied because of his great book, based on the series of lectures which he delivered at Harvard from 1911-16 – *Printing Types, Their History, Forms and Use; a Study in Survivals*. This is more than a scholarly history of the types themselves; it relates the history of printing to the background and civilization from which it sprang, and is infused throughout by the humane mind of its distinguished author. Its influence on good printers has been incalculable.

The Grabhorn Press gives us an endearing picture of achievement on a human scale in an increasingly mechanized world. It was founded in San Francisco in 1920 by two brothers, Edwin and Robert Grabhorn, who worked together in such harmony that it has been said of them: 'When Ed's

118 *(opposite)* One of the best of the Nonesuch Press's many books is Dante's *Divina Commedia*, with the exquisite drawings by Botticelli. Italian and English texts are printed in parallel columns in the same italic type. Sir Francis Meynell had a theory that by slowing the reader's eye, this type increased his capacity to absorb the beauty of the text

117 *(below)* The first advertisement issued by the brothers Edwin and Robert Grabhorn when they opened their printing house in San Francisco in 1920

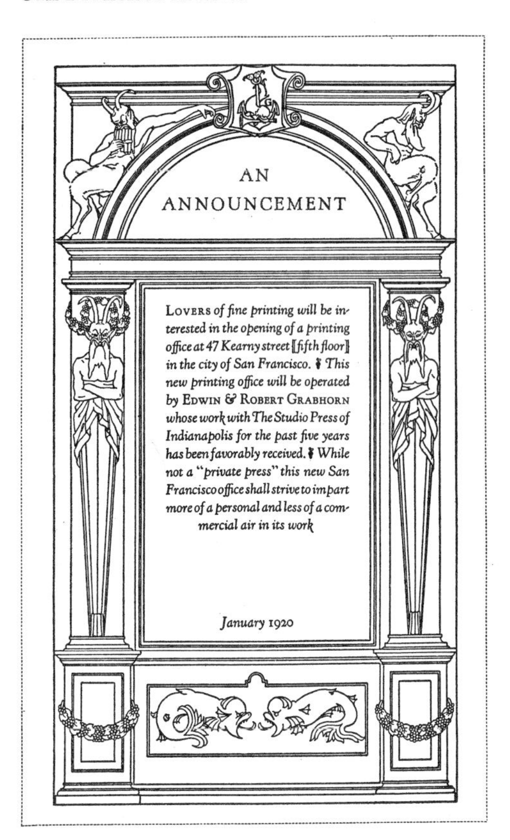

away the shop goes to pieces; when Bob's away Ed goes to pieces.' Their first workshop occupied the fifth floor of humble premises in a narrow street, and they supported themselves by doing all manner of general, and even jobbing printing, until their reputation brought the support which enabled them to embark on their stately folios. Perhaps the most distinguished of these is Whitman's *Leaves of Grass*, which 'occupied the entire resources of the press for well over a year'. At one point the Grabhorns considered stating in the colophon: 'Four hundred copies printed and the press destroyed.' Oscar Lewis, who was intimately connected with the press, has written a charming memoir, to be found in *The New Colophon*, Volume II, Part 5 (1949).

AN
ANNOUNCEMENT
Lovers of fine printing will be interested in the opening of a printing office at 47 Kearny street [fifth floor] in the city of San Francisco. ❦ This new printing office will be operated by Edwin & Robert Grabhorn whose work with The Studio Press of Indianapolis for the past five years has been favorably received. ❦ While not a "private press" this new San Francisco office shall strive to impart more of a personal and less of a commercial air in its work
January 1920

On the opposite wing of modern American fine printing lies the Limited Editions Club, founded in 1929, inspired and conducted by George Macy. This may be compared to the Nonesuch Press, for its aim has been to make fine books available at comparatively reasonable prices. Owing to the size and affluence of America, patronage exists there on a scale without precedent in the history of fine printing, and in its first quarter of a century the Limited Editions Club issued 250 books for its 1500 members. To this end it has commissioned work not only from American printers such as the Merrymount Press, the Grabhorn Press, William E. Rudge, Henry Nash and others, but also from European countries – the Golden Cockerel Press and the Oxford University Press in England, J. Enschedé in Holland, Hans Mardersteig of the Officina Bodoni in Italy, etc. In the *Gulliver* which he designed for them, Bruce Rogers was given an opportunity to display a rare sense of humour in a charming *jeu d'esprit*, in which *Voyage to Lilliput* measures $2^1/_2$ by $3^3/_4$ inches, the *Voyage to Brobdingnag* $13^1/_2$ by 18 inches [figure 119].

The illustrators commissioned by George Macy display a far more adventurous taste than that of the English private presses, which relied too parochially on the Pre-Raphaelites and the Arts and Crafts movement. In addition to American and British artists, Limited Editions Club books have been illustrated by George Grosz, Marie Laurencin, Matisse and Picasso. Picasso produced pencil drawings and etchings for the *Lysistrata* of Aristophanes (in an excellent translation by Gilbert Seldes), while Matisse illustrated James Joyce's *Ulysses*. Writing about the inception of this commission, George Macy records:

> I have never been more greatly impressed with the mental facility of an artist than I was when I suggested to Matisse that he should illustrate *Ulysses*. He said, over the telephone, that he had never read it. I got Stuart Gilbert to send him a copy of Mr. Gilbert's translation into French. The very next morning, M. Matisse reported that he had read the book, that he understood its eighteen episodes to be parodies of similar episodes in the *Odyssey*, that he would like to give point to this fact by making his illustrations actually illustrations of the original episodes in Homer! I may have been taken in, of course. If I was not, it can surely be said that Henri Matisse grasped this book quicker than any other man ever did.

With the success of the Nonesuch Press and the Limited Editions Club, the mission of the private presses was virtually achieved. Perceptive and sensitive publishers took note of what had been done and the standards of design and craftsmanship rose immeasurably; scores of excellent books poured into the bookshops. Under the guidance of Stanley Morison the Monotype Corporation produced a series of fine types, including one of the greatest ever cut – Times roman. In this type attractive books of every kind have been printed and it has been extensively used in paperbacks. The same happy state of affairs is to be seen in other countries; but I hope it will not seem chauvinistic to claim that the modern movement for the betterment of printing was in its inception an English one. The best books of today do not look in the least like Kelmscotts, but without Morris they might never have been created at all.

119 *(below) Gulliver's Travels*, as designed by Bruce Rogers for the Limited Editions Club, New York, in 1950, provides a problem for those collectors who, like Samuel Pepys, arrange their books in order of size!

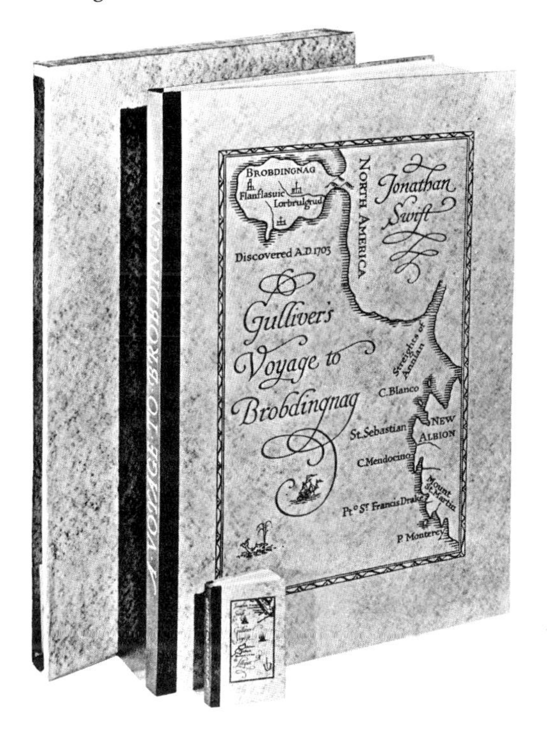

Bibliography

PRINTING

MCMURTRIE, D.C. *The Book. The Story of Printing and Bookmaking.* (Oxford University Press) 1943

STEINBERG, S. H. *Five Hundred Years of Printing.* (Pelican Books) 1955

ALDIS, H. G. *The Printed Book.* Second Edition. Revised by John Carter and Brooke Crutchley. (Cambridge University Press) 1947

CARTER, J. *ABC for Book Collectors.* Fourth Edition. (Rupert Hart-Davis) 1966

UPDIKE, D. B. *Printing Types, Their History, Forms, and Use. A Study in Survivals.* 2 vols. Second Edn. (Oxford University Press) 1937

SCHOLDERER, V. *Johann Gutenberg.* (British Museum) 1963

MANUSCRIPTS

RICKERT, M. *Painting in Britain in the Middle Ages.* (Pelican) 1954

– *The Reconstructed Carmelite Missal.* (Faber and Faber) 1952

PORCHER, J. *French Miniatures from Illuminated Manuscripts.* (Collins) 1960

SALMI, M. *Italian Miniatures.* (Collins) 1957

HARRISON, F. *English Manuscripts of the Fourteenth Century.* (Studio) 1937

MILLAR, E. G. *The Luttrell Psalter.* (British Museum) 1932

ALTON, E. H. and MEYER, P. (eds) *The Book of Kells.* Facsimile reproduction in colour. 3 vols. (Urs Graf) 1950-1

SULLIVAN, SIR E. *The Book of Kells.* (Studio) 1914

WARNER, SIR G. F. *Illuminated Manuscripts in the British Museum.* (British Museum) 1899-1903

Reproductions from Illuminated Manuscripts. Series 1 to 5. (British Museum) 1907-65

TURNER, D. H. *Early Gothic Illuminated Manuscripts in England.* (British Museum) 1965

– *Romanesque Illuminated Manuscripts in the British Museum.* (British Museum) 1966

VALENTINE, L. N. *Ornament in Mediaeval Manuscripts.* (Faber and Faber) 1965

COLOUR PLATE BOOKS

PRIDEAUX, S. T. *Aquatint Engraving.* (Duckworth) 1909

TOOLEY, R. V. *English Books with Coloured Plates, 1790 to 1860.* (Batsford) 1954

ABBEY, J. R. *Scenery of Great Britain and Ireland in Aquatint and Lithography, 1770-1860.* 1952

– *Life in England in Aquatint and Lithography, 1770-1860.* 1953

– *Travel in Aquatint and Lithography, 1770-1860.* 1956-7

GREGO, F. *Thomas Rowlandson.* 2 vols. 1880

BLAND, D. *A History of Book Illustration.* (Faber and Faber) 1958

PRIVATE PRESSES

TOMKINSON, SIR G. S. *A Select Bibliography of the Principle Modern Presses, Public and Private in Great Britain and Ireland.* (First Edition Club) 1928

MORRIS, W. *A Note on His Aims in Founding the Kelmscott Press, with Bibliography.* (Kelmscott Press) 1898

MACKAIL, J. W. *The Life of William Morris.* 2 vols. (Longmans) 1899

SPARLING, H. H. *The Kelmscott Press and William Morris.* (Macmillan) 1924

Catalogue Raisonné of Books Printed at The Doves Press, 1916

Descriptive Bibliography of Books Printed at the Ashendene Press, 1935

Nonesuch Century, (The). Edited by A. J. A. Symons and others. 1936.

Golden Cockerel Press Bibliographies: Chanticleer, 1921-36; *Pertelote,* 1936-43; *Cockalorum,* 1943-9